INSTITUTE OF GEOLOGICAL SCIENCES
Natural Environment Research Council

GEMSTONES
IN THE
GEOLOGICAL
MUSEUM

A guide to the collection

By

W. F. P. McLINTOCK, CB, DSc
FOURTH EDITION

Revised by
PATRICIA M. STATHAM, BSc, FGA
Based on the Third Edition revision by
P. A. SABINE, DSc, ARCS

LONDON HER MAJESTY'S STATIONERY OFFICE 1983

*The Institute of Geological Sciences
was formed by the incorporation of the
Geological Survey of Great Britain
and the Geological Museum
with Overseas Geological Surveys
and is a constituent body of the
Natural Environment Research Council*

First edition 1912
Third edition March 1951
Fourth edition 1983

ISBN 0 11 884201 3

PREFACE TO FOURTH EDITION

Following the complete rearrangement of the gemstone exhibition it has become necessary to prepare a new edition of the Guide. Many new gem species have been added to the
collections in recent years and the displays of well-known gemstones have been aug-
mented. There has been a considerable expansion in the production of synthetic gemstones, and the proliferation of diamond simulants is noteworthy. These developments
have been incorporated into the new edition. Much of the general text in the previous
edition is still applicable and this has not been changed materially, though to assist the
modern reader it has been brought up to date wherever possible. In a developing world
the names of gem-producing countries may change rapidly, but many older names in the
text have been retained partly because such terms as Siam ruby and Ceylon sapphire are
still widely used. Some newer names (with the older name in brackets) are shown in the
following list: Sri Lanka (Ceylon), Malagasy Republic (Madagascar), Kampuchea
(Khmer Republic, Cambodia), Thailand (Siam), Namibia (South West Africa), Zaire
(Congo), Zimbabwe (Rhodesia).

With the involvement of Dr Sabine the guide has been revised by Miss P. M. Statham
under the supervision of Mr E. A. Jobbins.

G. M. BROWN
Director

Institute of Geological Sciences
Exhibition Road,
South Kensington
LONDON SW7 2DE
20 December 1981

PREFACE TO THIRD EDITION

Since the publication of the second edition of this Guide a quarter of a century ago, the transfer of the Museum from Jermyn Street to South Kensington in 1935 presented the opportunity to display the gemstones in a more fitting manner than before.

Along with those massive minerals which are used for ornamental purposes the gem minerals are arranged in a series of exhibits in the Main Hall of the Museum and this edition of the Guide describes them as they are now displayed. Descriptions of the principal additions to the collection have been introduced and some of the old diagrams have been replaced by new drawings of a more suitable character.

The Guide has been revised by Mr Sabine under the supervision of Dr Phemister who has acted as Editor.

W. F. P. McLintock
Director

Geological Museum
South Kensington
London SW7
31 October 1950

PREFACE TO FIRST EDITION

The Museum of Practical Geology has acquired at various times by purchase, donation, and bequest, not only specimens of all the more important minerals used for purposes of personal adornment, but also specimens illustrating methods of cutting and polishing the natural stones so as to enhance their beauty. Following the general practice of this Museum, examples of these gemstones as found in nature, and as prepared for the jeweller, together with a few specimens of the jewellers' art, have been brought together and, for many years, have formed one of our most useful and attractive exhibits.

The gemstones to which the Guide refers, form a part of a general collection illustrating the uses of the so-called non-metallic minerals. They have not been arranged in special cases, but the references in the Guide will enable any of them to be easily found. For the benefit of students and the public, brief accounts of the general properties, of the methods employed in cutting and identification, and of the imitation, treatment, and artificial formation of gemstones have been given.

Great interest has been aroused of late years in the artificial preparation of such minerals as ruby, sapphire, and spinel. Some examples of these artificial gems will be found in the cases, side by side with the natural products, and not the least interesting part of the Guide is that which refers to these artificial stones and to the processes by which they have been obtained.

The Guide has been written by Mr McLintock, under the supervision of Mr Howe, who has acted as Editor.

J. J. H. Teall
Director

Museum of Practical Geology
Jermyn Street
29 March 1912

CONTENTS

1   Introduction   1
2   Properties of gemstones   3
3   Cutting of gemstones   19
4   Imitation, treatment and artificial
    formation of gemstones   24
5   Description of gemstones displayed
    in the collection   31
Appendix: Identification tables   74
Index   78

Figures

1   Plan of the Gemstone
    Collection   vi
2   Refraction of light in a stone   8
3   Total internal reflection of light in
    a stone   9
4   Diamond   9
5   Quartz   10
6   Path of rays in a brilliant   10
7   Dispersion of white light by a
    transparent prism   11
8   Dispersion and total internal
    reflection of light in a brilliant   11
9   Principle of the refractometer   13
10 The appearance of a refractometer
    scale with a singly refracting
    stone   13
11 The appearance of a refractometer
    scale with a doubly refracting
    stone   13
12 The dichroscope   15
13 The brilliant   20
14 The step cut   20
15 The rose cut   21
16 The briolette   21
17 The marquise   21
18 The pendeloque   21
19 Simple cabochon   22
20 Double cabochon   22
21 Hollow cabochon   22
22 Inverted blowpipe apparatus   28
23 Octahedral crystal of
    diamond   32
24 Dodecahedral crystal of
    diamond   32
25 Cubic crystal of diamond   32
26 Rhombic dodecahedron   49
27 Icositetrahedron   49
28 Group of quartz crystals   63

Plates

1   Corundum   Facing p. 42
2   Beryl group   Facing p. 42
3   Olivine (peridot), spinel, chrysoberyl
    and sinhalite   Facing p. 43
4   Topaz and tourmaline   Facing p. 43
5   Zircon   Facing p. 58
6   Jade   Facing p. 58
7   Opal group   Facing p. 59
8   Quartz group   Facing p. 59

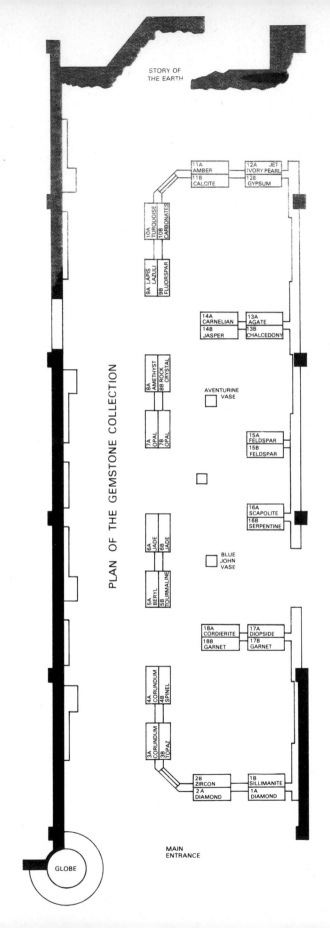

Figure 1 Plan of the Gemstone Collection

PLAN OF THE GEMSTONE COLLECTION

STORY OF THE EARTH

11A AMBER
11B CALCITE
12A JET IVORY PEARL
12B GYPSUM

10A TURQUOISE
10B CARBONATES

9A LAPIS LAZULI
9B FLUORSPAR

14A CARNELIAN
14B JASPER
13A AGATE
13B CHALCEDONY

8A AMETHYST
8B ROCK CRYSTAL

AVENTURINE VASE

7A OPAL
7B OPAL

15A FELDSPAR
15B FELDSPAR

16A SCAPOLITE
16B SERPENTINE

6A JADE
6B JADE

BLUE JOHN VASE

5A BERYL
5B TOURMALINE

18A CORDIERITE
18B GARNET
17A DIOPSIDE
17B GARNET

4A CORUNDUM
4B SPINEL

3A CORUNDUM
3B TOPAZ

2B ZIRCON
2A DIAMOND
1B SILLIMANITE
1A DIAMOND

GLOBE

MAIN ENTRANCE

1 INTRODUCTION

The minerals in the Geological Museum are arranged for the most part according to their commercial applications, so that the ores (minerals used for the extraction of metals), are separated from the non-metallic minerals which are generally not used for this purpose. This arrangement has, of course, no scientific basis and fails to bring out the relationships between the various species, but it has the advantage of showing those minerals which are concerned with commerce and mining in a compact and accessible way.

The term non-metallic is misleading as it is applied to nearly all the minerals which contain one or more metals, but usually to the light metals, e.g. aluminium, calcium, magnesium, potassium, sodium, as opposed to the heavy metals of commerce, such as copper, tin, silver, gold, lead, etc.

Amongst the non-metallic minerals gemstones occupy an important place from the point of view of commercial and general interest. Because of this, they have been brought together to occupy the cases in the centre of the ground floor of the Museum. Usually gemstones show no natural relationships with one another, the only feature which unites them into a class being their suitability for decorative use. This suitability depends mainly on *beauty* and *durability*. Many stones possessing these qualities in a high degree have, however, little or no value at the present time, for there is a wide distinction between a stone naturally fitted for the purposes of the jeweller, and one for which there is a demand.

From the commercial point of view the really precious stones are *diamond, ruby, sapphire, emerald*, and *opal*. (The *pearl*, although among the most valuable gems can hardly be termed a mineral but is included.) The demand for these is fairly constant and the value of good specimens is always high. The fashion of the moment dictates the value of the other minerals which legitimately claim a place among gemstones. At one time it may be *tourmaline*, at another, *peridot*, at another, *cat's-eye*, or *aquamarine*, or *topaz*, or *zircon*, which is in vogue; the favoured gem consequently rises in value until some new whim relegates it to comparative obscurity. To such stones 'semi-precious' is sometimes applied, although the use of this term is to be deprecated, as it frequently casts a stigma upon beautiful and rare stones.

The element of rarity plays, perhaps, the most important part in determining the value of a gemstone and outweighs, by what often seems a disproportionate amount, considerations of beauty and of durability. In this respect it must be noted that, although a particular mineral may be fairly abundant, yet pieces suitable for cutting are usually rare. The *emerald*, one of the most valuable stones at present, provides a striking example. Crystals of emerald are not uncommon, but those possessing the correct colour combined with transparency and freedom from flaws are exceedingly rare and cut specimens of such perfect stones command very high prices.

The ruby gives an instructive example of the influence of rarity on values of precious stones.

This stone is manufactured in clear transparent finely coloured masses, (see p. 27) which, when cut and polished become very effective gems. These synthetic rubies are identical for all practical purposes with the natural stone and can only be distinguished from it by special examination, yet the difference in value between the two is enormous.

The artificial stone can be purchased for a pound or so per carat, whilst a Burmese stone of similar colour and transparency would fetch, because of its rarity, thousands of pounds per carat, the price per carat depending partly upon the weight.

The diamond, superior to all other natural stones in hardness, lustre and 'fire', is popularly supposed to stand first in value, yet because of the comparative abundance of good specimens, its value is often less than that of emerald and the ruby. So the possession of beauty and durability entitles a mineral to rank as a precious stone, whilst rarity, combined with these two characteristics, settles its position in the series.

Various classifications of precious stones have been adopted from time to time, but all are more or less unsatisfactory. In Chapter 5 the stones are considered in the order in which they occur in the cases (see Figure 1), starting with diamond. Chapter 2 deals with the properties of precious stones with special reference to their identification; in Chapter 3 the principal styles of cutting are touched upon; whilst Chapter 4 deals with the imitation, artificial treatment and formation of precious stones. Throughout the descriptions, the unit of weight used is the *metric carat* of one-fifth (0.2) gram. Approximately 28 grams equal one ounce avoirdupois.

In order to make the identification of cut specimens easier, the principal stones have been tabulated according to colour and other physical properties, and the tables will be found at the end of the book.

The literature relating to gemstones is wide and scattered; some books dealing with the subject are:

Anderson, B. W. 1971. *Gem Testing*. 8th edition.
Bruton, E. 1978. *Diamonds*. 2nd edition.
McCallien, W. J. 1937. *Scottish Gem Stones*.
Smith, G. F. H. 1972. *Gemstones*. 14th edition.
Spencer, L. J. 1946. *A Key to Precious Stones*. 2nd edition.
Sutton, J. R. 1928. *Diamond: A descriptive treatise*.
Tolansky, S. 1962. *The History and Use of Diamond*.
Webster, R. 1979. *The Gemmologists' Compendium*. 6th edition.
Webster, R. 1976. *Practical Gemmology*. 6th edition.
Webster, R. 1975. *Gems: Their Sources, Descriptions and Identification*. 3rd edition.
Williams, A. F. 1932. *The Genesis of the Diamond*. 2 vols.

Apart from these separate volumes many interesting and important papers are published in the quarterly *Journal of Gemmology and Proceedings of the Gemmological Association of Great Britain*.

2 PROPERTIES OF GEMSTONES

With long practice it is possible to train the eye to recognise the various members of this series of minerals with some precision; but anyone who inspects a collection of cut gems must be struck at once by the resemblance between different stones and the bewildering varieties of colour shown by the same species. It frequently happens that even the expert eye is at a loss and, in such cases tests must be carried out to confirm the identity of the specimen.

A knowledge of the properties of gemstones is also essential for a correct and intelligent appreciation of their beauty. To understand why stones should be faceted in certain ways; to know the best directions in which particular stones must be cut in order to get the maximum effect; to realise why, for instance, the diamond should be so incomparably superior to all other natural white stones in 'fire' and 'life'; these, and many other points, are made clear with the knowledge of a few fundamental facts.

The properties will be considered in the following order: Crystalline form; Hardness; Cleavage and fracture; Specific gravity; Optical properties; Thermal and electrical properties; Chemical properties.

Crystalline form

A study of the substances in the mineral kingdom shows that the majority of them occur in definite forms, or crystals, which are bounded by a series of planes known as faces. Investigation of the various kinds of crystals has resulted in their being divided into seven orders, or systems, called, respectively, the *Cubic*, the *Tetragonal*, the *Orthorhombic*, the *Hexagonal*, the *Trigonal*, the *Monoclinic*, and the *Triclinic* system. In each of these the faces are referred to directions or lines, known as *axes*, which, in the different systems, are differently related to one another. For an account of crystallography, or the science of crystals, the reader is referred to any of the numerous books on the subject. It must be pointed out here that the external form of a crystal is simply an expression of the definite internal structure or arrangement of the atoms which build up the whole. Gemstones, as a rule, are well crystallised and many of the interesting properties displayed by them—notably the effects which they produce on light—can be directly traced to their crystalline structure.

Hardness

Most precious stones have a high degree of hardness which may be defined as the power of resisting abrasion. To this they owe their durability and their power to take and to retain a high polish. Hardness is measured by comparison with certain selected minerals, a stone being harder than those which it can scratch and softer than those to which it yields. The scale generally used is that drawn up by Mohs and consists of the following ten minerals arranged in ascending order of hardness:

1	Talc	6	Feldspar
2	Gypsum	7	Quartz
3	Calcite	8	Topaz
4	Fluorspar	9	Corundum
5	Apatite	10	Diamond

In practice only the last five of this scale need to be used, as all the important gemstones possess a hardness of at least 5. Crystals or sharp fragments of the minerals 6–10 can be mounted on brass rods and used as 'hardness points' for testing specimens. If the stones are in the rough state the tests are easily made, but, if they are cut, great care is needed to prevent injury to any of the facets. The girdle is the most convenient place to use, as any mark made there is of no importance and will subsequently be hidden by the mount. Successive trials are made with the test minerals until a scratch is made on the stone, and from this an idea of the hardness is obtained. Thus, if the specimen resists quartz but yields to topaz, its hardness lies between 7 and 8, and is designated as about $7\frac{1}{2}$. A common error in making this examination is to mistake for a scratch the streak left when a softer mineral is rubbed over a harder one, and it is advisable to rub the mark and examine the place with a lens.

A more convenient way in which to test the hardness of cut stones, is to use polished plates of the minerals 6 – 9 and to rub the gem successively over them, beginning with the number 6, until no scratch is obtained.

It must not be imagined that the intervals between members of Mohs' scale are of equal value and that the difference between talc and gypsum is the same as that between corundum and diamond. As a matter of fact diamond is so superior to all other minerals in this respect that the difference between it and corundum is very much greater than that between any other minerals on the scale.

Ordinary window-glass has a hardness of about 5 and can be readily scratched by all true gemstones as well as by a steel file, so that it is a simple matter to determine whether a specimen is genuine or merely an imitation in glass, but this determination must be carried out with great care or damage may easily be done to genuine stones.

Table 1 Order of hardness

Diamond	10	Spodumene	7–$6\frac{1}{2}$	Diopside	6–5
Corundum	9	Kyanite	7–5	Scapolite	6–5
Chrysoberyl	$8\frac{1}{2}$	Idocrase	$6\frac{1}{2}$	Enstatite	$5\frac{1}{2}$
Spinel	8	Cassiterite	$6\frac{1}{2}$	Sphene	$5\frac{1}{2}$
Taaffeite	8	Olivine	$6\frac{1}{2}$	Brazilianite	$5\frac{1}{2}$
Topaz	8	Kornerupine	$6\frac{1}{2}$	Lazulite	$5\frac{1}{2}$
Phenakite	$7\frac{3}{4}$	Sinhalite	$6\frac{1}{2}$	Apatite	5
Beryl	$7\frac{3}{4}$	Zoisite	$6\frac{1}{2}$	Datolite	5
Euclase	$7\frac{1}{2}$	Ekanite	$6\frac{1}{2}$	Fluorspar	4
Andalusite	$7\frac{1}{2}$	Epidote	$6\frac{1}{2}$	Sphalerite	4–$3\frac{1}{2}$
Sillimanite	$7\frac{1}{2}$	Chalcedony	$6\frac{1}{2}$	Serpentine	4–$2\frac{1}{2}$
Hambergite	$7\frac{1}{2}$	Benitoite	$6\frac{1}{2}$	Phosphophyllite	$3\frac{1}{2}$
Zircon	$7\frac{1}{2}$–6	Nephrite	$6\frac{1}{2}$–$5\frac{1}{2}$	Calcite	3
Garnet	$7\frac{1}{2}$–6	Feldspar	6	Jet	3
Cordierite	$7\frac{1}{2}$–7	Turquoise	6	Amber	$2\frac{1}{2}$
Tourmaline	$7\frac{1}{4}$	Amblygonite	6	Gypsum	2
Quartz	7	Beryllonite	6	Meerschaum	2
Danburite	7	Opal	6	Talc	1
Jadeite	7–$6\frac{1}{2}$	Sodalite	6		
Axinite	7–$6\frac{1}{2}$	Lapis-lazuli	6		

Table 1 lists the principal stones arranged in order of hardness. It will be noted that in several cases the value varies between limits. This is because crystals possess different degrees of hardness in different directions, but the differences in most cases are so slight that they cannot be detected by the methods of testing described above. The mineral *kyanite*, however, is exceptional, for here the difference is so great that it is quite evident in ordinary tests (p. 46).

Cleavage and fracture

Crystals possess different cohesion in different directions and frequently show a tendency to split or cleave along certain planes when subjected to a blow. Thus the diamond splits very easily parallel to the faces of the octahedron; topaz, parallel to the basal plane; fluorspar, parallel to the octahedral faces, as in diamond; and so on. Many gemstones, however, e.g. tourmaline, spinel, garnet, corundum, etc., show little or no trace of cleavage, and, when broken, present a conchoidal fracture.

Cleavage is not a property by which faceted stones may be identified, but it is of great importance in the process of cutting and renders the operation in the case of the diamond much easier than it would be otherwise.

Specific gravity

The ratio of the weight of a body to that of an equal volume of pure water is termed the specific gravity, and, as this number is constant and definite for any one species of stone, its determination offers a reliable means of identifying cut specimens without injury to them. Thus any piece of ruby is found to weigh four times as much as an equal volume of water, i.e. the specific gravity of ruby is 4. By a well-known principle, a body, when immersed in water, loses in weight an amount equal to the weight of the water displaced, and, as the volume of water displaced is clearly equal to that of the immersed body, it offers a convenient method of determining specific gravity. This comprises weighing the body in air and then in water; the loss gives the weight of water displaced, i.e. the weight of a volume of water occupying the same space as the body, and this, divided into the weight in air, gives the specific gravity of the body.

An accurate method of determining this is with a chemical balance The gemstone is first weighed in air, and then, suspended in a fine wire cage, in water. After allowance has been made for the weight of the wire, the specific gravity of the stone is easily calculable.

Let the weight of the stone in air		= 2.1543 g
and the weight of the stone in water suspended in a wire cage	= 1.3630 g	
The weight of the wire cage alone in water	= 0.0033 g	
Then weight of stone alone in water	= 1.3597 g	= 1.3597 g
Loss in weight		= 0.7946 g

and the specific gravity $= \dfrac{\text{weight in air}}{\text{loss in weight}} = \dfrac{2.1543}{0.7946} = 2.71$

Heavy solutions may also be used to determine specific gravity. A body floats in a liquid of higher specific gravity than itself and sinks in one of lower specific gravity; in a liquid of the same specific gravity it neither floats nor sinks but simply remains suspended. The liquids most generally utilised are 1 bromoform, which has a specific gravity of 2.9 at ordinary temperatures; 2 methylene iodide, which has a specific gravity of 3.33 at ordinary temperatures; 3 Clerici solution, which is a concentrated solution of thallium formate and malonate and has a maximum specific gravity of about 4.2. It is a colourless viscous liquid which may be diluted with water, is very expensive, and is poisonous. The other two liquids, which may be diluted with toluene or alcohol, should be kept in the dark, as they become coloured on exposure to light. These chemicals should be used with great care and Clerici solution must not be allowed to come into contact with the skin.

In practice it is often sufficient to know that the specific gravity of a stone lies between certain limits, and for this purpose the following set of solutions is recommended:

		Specific gravity
1	Clerici solution diluted to	4.0
2	Clerici solution diluted to	3.52
3	Methylene iodide	3.33
4	Methylene iodide diluted to	3.06
5	Bromoform	2.9
6	Bromoform diluted to	2.71
7	Bromoform diluted to	2.65

Table 2   Principal stones arranged in order of specific gravity

GGG	7.05	Sphene	3.53–3.45	Prehnite	2.94–2.88
Cassiterite	7.0–6.8	Diamond	3.53–3.51	Lapis-lazuli	2.9–2.7
Scheelite	6.1	Epidote	3.5–3.35	Beryl	2.90–2.68
Cubic zirconia	5.7	Sinhalite	3.49–3.46	Beryllonite	2.84–2.80
Strontium titanate	5.13	Olivine	3.46–3.35	Turquoise	2.8–2.6
Zircon	4.7–3.94	Idocrase	3.4–3.3	Pearl	2.78–2.60
Lithium niobate	4.64	Jadeite	3.4–3.3	Calcite	2.71
YAG	4.57	Zoisite	3.35	Labradorite	2.70–2.66
Almandine	4.3–3.9	Kornerupine	3.32–3.27	Scapolite	2.70–2.63
Rutile	4.26–4.18	Diopside	3.31–3.27	Sunstone	2.67–2.65
Spessartine	4.20–4.12	Axinite	3.29–3.27	Quartz	2.65
Sphalerite	4.10–4.08	Enstatite	3.27–3.1	Cordierite	2.65–2.58
Corundum	4.01–3.99	Sillimanite	3 25–3.23	Chalcedony	2.63–2.58
Demantoid	3.86–3.81	Apatite	3.22–3.17	Moonstone	2.57–2.56
Pyrope	3.8–3.7	Spodumene	3.20–3.15	Orthoclase	2.57–2.55
Chrysoberyl	3.74–3.64	Andalusite	3.18–3.12	Amazonstone	2.57–2.55
Rhodochrosite	3.70–3.45	Fluorspar	3.18–3.02	Hambergite	2.4–2.35
Benitoite	3.68–3.64	Tourmaline	3.15–3.00	Sodalite	2.35–2.15
Kyanite	3.68–3.65	Euclase	3.10–3.05	Opal	2.2–1.9
Hessonite	3.65–3.63	Amblygonite	3.03–3.01	Meerschaum	2.0–1.0
Spinel	3.65–3.58	Danburite	3.00	Ivory (elephant)	1.90–1.70
Taaffeite	3.61–3.60	Datolite	3.00–2.9		
Topaz	3.56–3.50	Nephrite	3.0–2.9	Jet	1.35–1.30
		Brazilianite	2.99–2.98	Amber	1.1–1.05
		Phenakite	2.97–2.95		

The liquid of specific gravity 2.65 may be prepared by diluting bromoform until a small piece of quartz placed in it as a marker remains suspended. Calcite, green tourmaline, diamond and synthetic corundum may similarly be used as markers for the liquids of specific gravity 2.71, 3.06, 3.52 and 4.0 respectively. As they are pure liquids, bromoform, of specific gravity 2.9, and methylene iodide, of specific gravity 3.33, do not require markers.

By observing the behaviour of a stone in these solutions, starting with that of lowest specific gravity, the stone can often be identified without further trouble.

Optical properties

Lustre, brilliancy, fire, colour, in fact, all the qualities which go to make up the beauty of precious stones, are directly due to the powerful influence which they exert upon reflected and transmitted light. Stones seldom occur in nature in a form suitable for showing such properties to advantage, and it is the business of the cutter to treat the rough specimen in the manner best calculated to display its latent beauties. A knowledge of the optical properties is essential to do this in an intelligent way. This knowledge offers a reliable method of identifying cut stones without injuring them in any way. The optical properties characteristic of gemstones are conveniently classed as follows:

Transparency, lustre, refraction, dispersion, double refraction, colour, dichroism and spectroscopic properties; a few stones, such as *opal, moonstone, cat's-eye*, etc., depend for their beauty on special optical effects which will be noted under a separate heading (p. 16).

Transparency   Stones are called transparent, translucent and opaque, in accordance with the amount of light which penetrates them. When an object is viewed through a transparent stone its outlines are clear and sharp, when through a semi-transparent one, blurred and indistinct. Translucent stones allow a certain amount of light to pass through but no image of an object can be obtained, whilst opaque stones allow no light to pass at all. Most gemstones are extremely transparent except when marred by flaws which greatly impair their transparency and cause a large reduction in value. *Opal* (Case 7) may be mentioned as an example of a translucent stone, whilst *turquoise* (Case 10A) is opaque. It must, of course, be understood that these terms apply to cut speci-mens of ordinary thickness and that most minerals are transparent or, at least, translucent when in sufficiently thin pieces.

The behaviour of gemstones towards X-rays has been investigated, and it has been found that different stones show different degrees of transparency to these radiations. Thus *diamond* and *phenakite* are quite transparent; *corundum* (includ-ing *ruby* and *sapphire*) is transparent, but not to the same extent as the two former stones; *chrysoberyl* and *opal* are still less transparent; *quartz, topaz, feldspar, diopside*, and *spodumene* are translucent; *turquoise, tourmaline, peridot*, and *sphene* are almost opaque; whilst *almandine, beryl, zircon, epidote* and *glass* are opaque. When some stones, notably pale yellow corundum, are exposed to a strong concentration of X-rays, their colour may be deepened, but this effect is usually only temporary and the colour fades again in a few hours on exposure to light.

Lustre   This is essentially a surface effect and is due to the reflection which always takes place when light strikes a bright surface. The highest kind of lustre is that shown by polished metal and is known as metallic lustre, but it occurs only on opaque substances and is possessed by no gemstone of importance. The other kinds of lustre recognised are adamantine, as in the *diamond*; vitreous, as in *ruby, sapphire*, and most precious stones; resinous, as in some kinds of *garnet*; silky, as in *cat's-eye, satin-spar*, and several minerals showing a fibrous structure; pearly, as shown by the cleavage faces of *topaz* and *feldspar*; and *waxy*, as in the *turquoise*.

Refraction   When light from outside strikes the surface of a transparent body a certain amount is reflected whilst a certain amount penetrates the substance. In the latter case the light does not preserve its original path, but is bent or refracted, and proceeds on its way in a new direction. The power of refracting light is strong in many gemstones, and several of the beautiful effects for which they are renowned are attributed to it.

Figure 2   Refraction of light in a stone

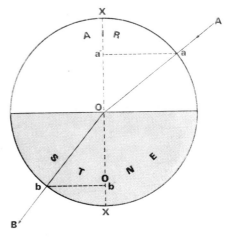

Figure 2 represents a ray of light A O travelling from air into a transparent precious stone. XOX' is drawn perpendicular to the surface of separation, O B represents the path of the ray in the stone; it has been bent towards the perpendicular line and lies in the plane containing O A and XOX'. If a circle is drawn with O as centre and the lines aa' and bb' drawn perpendicular to XOX'; then aa'/bb' is a measure of the refracting power of the stone and is called the refractive index. The refractive index is independent of the size of the angle XOA. This angle is called the angle of incidence, and, in the case of light travelling from air into an optically denser medium, it is always greater than the angle of refraction, X'OB, from which it follows that aa' is always greater than bb', i.e. the refractive index is always greater than 1.

If light travels from a stone into air (Figure 3) the ray is again deviated but, in this case, it is bent away from the perpendicular, i.e. the angle X'OA is less than the angle XOB. If, as shown in the figure, the angle X'OA is increased, a point is reached—represented by X'OA²—when the emergent light (O B²) just grazes the surface of the stone, and if the angle X'OA is increased by very little beyond this—represented by X'OA³—no light emerges into the air, but is all thrown back into the stone (O B³). This phenomenon is called total internal reflection and the angle X'OA², i.e. the angle of incidence in the stone for which the emergent light grazes the bounding surface, is called the critical angle. This angle may also be defined as the angle of incidence at which total internal reflection begins, and it varies with the refracting power of the medium in which

Figure 3 Total internal
reflection of light in a stone

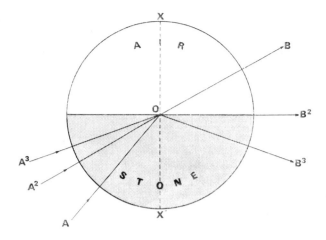

the light is travelling; thus, the greater the refractive index of a stone the smaller
is the critical angle, and *vice versa*. Figures 4 and 5 illustrate this point. In the case
of diamond (Figure 4) all rays which strike the bounding surface at an angle of
incidence greater than 24° 21' are reflected back into the stone. If there were a
whole series of rays travelling in the quadrant XOY and incident at O on the
boundary at all possible angles, a very large proportion of them, represented by
the more deeply shaded area, would not escape into the air. With quartz (Figure
5) light in order to undergo total reflection, must be incident at an angle greater
than 40° 8', so that if there were a series of rays travelling in the quadrant XOY,
a proportion of them, much smaller than in the previous case, would be totally
reflected.

Figure 4 Diamond: all rays incident at an
angle greater than 24°21' suffer total internal
reflection

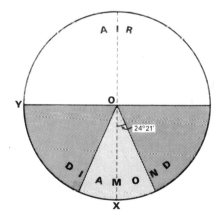

The brilliancy and life of a diamond cut in the brilliant style, especially when
viewed by top light, are due largely to total internal reflection. Owing to the
high refractive index, and consequent small critical angle of this stone, a beam of
light, once it has entered, experiences several reflections before it can emerge.

Figure 5   Quartz: all rays incident at an angle greater than 40°8′ suffer total internal reflection

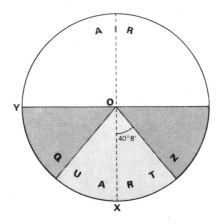

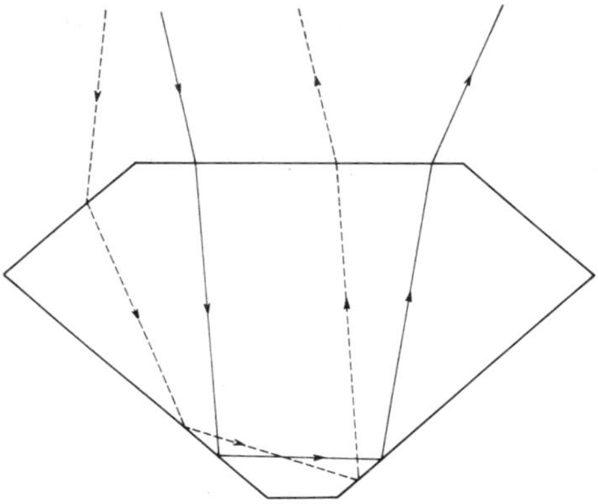

Figure 6   Path of rays in a brilliant

Figure 6 represents this diagrammatically. Light entering by the top facets is refracted and proceeds to the bottom ones which are steep; the angle of incidence of the beam is greater than the critical angle, and no light escapes into the air, but is all thrown back on to another facet when the process is repeated continually until the beam finally emerges by one of the top facets. The result of these reflections is that the stone is filled with light and the bottom facets appear like flashing mirrors.

Dispersion   White light is really composite, being made up of rays of the different colours seen in the spectrum. These colours are violet, indigo, blue, green, yellow, orange, red, and the rays to which they correspond are refracted to different extents. Thus it is found for any one stone the refractive index for blue light is greater than the refractive index for green light, which in turn is greater than that for yellow light, and so on. If, as shown in Figure 7, a beam of white light is passed through a prism of a transparent substance it is split up into its component parts owing to the rays of different colours being deviated to different amounts; the blue rays are more strongly refracted and deviated than the yellow ones, and these are more strongly deviated than the red ones, with the result that a series of colours is obtained if the emergent rays are thrown upon a white screen. This phenomenon is known as dispersion, and the power

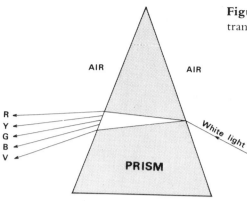

Figure 7 Dispersion of white light by a transparent prism

of so splitting up light is called dispersive power, which varies in different stones. It is strong in the diamond which, with a refractive index of 2.451 for violet light, and 2.407 for red light, has a dispersion of 0.044. Thus, when white light enters a diamond its component rays are widely separated and so the beautiful play of prismatic hues, known as fire, is obtained. In this respect diamond is superior to all other natural stones, for not only is the dispersion strong, but, owing to the high refractive index, the path of a beam of light emitted by a cut specimen is, as we have seen, a very long one, and the separation of the rays is consequently increased. Figure 8 illustrates this point.

Figure 8 Dispersion and total internal reflection of light in a brilliant

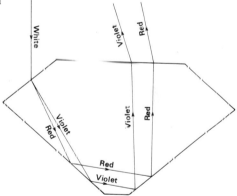

Other stones possessing strong dispersion are sphene (p. 48) and green garnet (p. 51). The fine green sphene in Case 1B admirably shows the strong dispersion, displaying particularly well flashes of red light which may be seen at night or even in dull weather from the gallery above.

Double refraction   The preceding notes on refraction apply to substances like glass, and to precious stones like diamond, garnet, and spinel which crystallise in the cubic system. A ray of light entering any of these is refracted and emerges as a single ray, and consequently any object such as a black spot or a candle flame appears single when viewed through them. Such substances are said to be singly refracting.

In minerals belonging to the other six crystallographic systems the incident ray is, in general, split up into two rays which take different paths and for which the refractive indices are different; a black spot or a flame when viewed through them appears double, and they are said to be doubly refracting.

It has already been pointed out that, when white light is refracted through a prism of a transparent substance, it is split up into its component colours, so that if, for example, a candle is viewed through such a prism, the image is fringed with colour. If the prism consists of a single refracting substance, one coloured image is obtained, but if the substance is doubly refracting, two coloured images are obtained.

The mineral calcite (Case 11B) offers the best illustration of double refraction as the separation of the two rays in this mineral is unusually great. The phenomenon is particularly well displayed by one specimen in the calcite case: a black cross, placed beneath a large cleavage block of Iceland spar, is seen from above as two distinct crosses. In most gemstones the images are not so widely separated and it is sometimes difficult to decide by the eye alone whether a specimen is doubly refracting or not.

The most satisfactory way of determining whether a specimen is or is not doubly refracting is to examine it between two Nicol prisms or plates of 'Polaroid'. Both Nicol prisms—so called after their inventor—which are cut from calcite, and 'polaroid' have the property of polarising light, and may be termed polarisers. A complete account of this phenomenon cannot be attempted here, but it may be said that if two Nicol prisms or plates of polaroid are held before the eye, and the one next to the observer is rotated, whilst the other is kept stationary, darkness occurs in two positions during a complete rotation. The light going through the first prism or plate has been so affected or polarised that it cannot go through the second one when it occupies one or other of these two positions. These positions lie at 180° from each other and in them the prisms or polaroids are referred to as crossed. Nicol prisms or polaroid plates are made use of in petrological microscopes, one being placed beneath the stage and one above. When a singly refracting specimen is placed between crossed polarisers and rotated, the field of view always remains dark; if, however, a doubly refracting stone is used darkness only occurs in four positions during a complete rotation. These four positions occur at intervals of 90°, and in all intermediate positions light gets through. Two points must be made. Firstly glass and singly refracting minerals may show 'anomalous double-refraction' due to strains existing internally. In such cases the positions of light and darkness are not nearly so well defined as in a true, doubly refracting specimen. In the second place doubly refracting stones all possess certain directions known as optic axes, and light travelling along these is not doubly refracted. Minerals belonging to the tetragonal, hexagonal and trigonal systems have one such direction and are hence called uniaxial, whilst those belonging to the orthorhombic, monoclinic, and triclinic systems have two such directions, and are called biaxial.

Always examine a specimen in several directions before concluding that it is singly refracting, as a totally wrong conclusion can be made as the result of viewing a doubly refracting stone along an optic axis.

Singly refracting stones have one definite refractive index, whilst doubly refracting stones have a series of refractive indices depending on the direction in which the light is travelling in them. These refractive indices vary between a maximum and minimum value. The difference in the values of the maximum and minimum refractive indices is called the double refraction or birefringence.

Figure 9 Principle of the refractometer

AB   surface of hemisphere
NN   normal
G   gemstone
L   lenses
S   scale
P   totally reflecting
      prism
I   incident ray
R   reflected ray

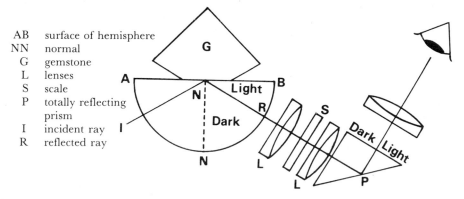

The determination of the refractive index is a valuable method of identifying a cut specimen, and an instrument called a refractometer is used by means of which the refractive index or indices can be read off directly from a scale seen through the eyepiece. Refractometers consist of a glass prism—or hemisphere in some types of instrument—of high refractive index (Figure 9) mounted flat side upwards, on which a flat polished facet of the gemstone to be tested is placed. Optical continuity is ensured by putting a drop of oil, also of high refractive index, between the two. Light is passed through the prism and at the interface between the glass and the gemstone, provided the stone is of lower refractive index than the glass, total internal reflection occurs if the angle of incidence is greater than the critical angle. Light incident at an angle less than the critical angle will be refracted out through the gemstone as described above (p. 12) When the reflected light is viewed through the eye-piece, part of the field is light where the light has been reflected and part of the field is dark where the light has been refracted out through the gemstone. The position of the sharp shadow edge has a regular relation to the refractive index which consequently may be read on a scale seen, with the shadow edge, through the eyepiece (Figure 10).

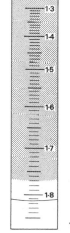

Figure 10 The appearance of a refractometer scale with a singly refracting stone

Figure 11 The appearance of a refractometer scale with a doubly refracting stone

For doubly refracting stones two shadow edges are, in general, seen lying close together (Figure 11), representing the two refractive indices. The faint shadow edge shown in Figures 10 and 11 at 1.812 is caused by the oil of that refractive index used between the stone and the glass prism.

Table 3   Stones arranged according to refractive indices

Singly refracting stones

Diamond	2.42	YAG	1.83	Spinel	1.72
Sphalerite	2.37	Almandine	1.75–1.81	Ekanite	1.60
Cubic zirconia	2.18	Spessartine	1.80	Sodalite	1.48
GGG	2.02	Pyrope	1.74–1.75	Opal	1.45
Demantoid	1.90	Hessonite	1.74	Fluorspar	1.43

Doubly refracting stones

	Maximum	Minimum		Maximum	Minimum
Rutile	2.90	2.62	Enstatite	1.67	1.66
Lithium niobate	2.30	2.21	Euclase	1.67	1.65
Cassiterite	2.09	1.99	Jadeite	1.67	1.65
Sphene	2.06	1.91	Datolite	1.67	1.63
Zircon (normal)	1.99	1.92	Turquoise	1.65	1.61
Scheelite	1.94	1.92	Apatite	1.64	1.64
Benitoite	1.80	1.76	Andalusite	1.64	1.63
Corundum	1.77	1.76	Danburite	1.64	1.63
Epidote	1.77	1.73	Tourmaline	1.64	1.62
Chrysoberyl	1.76	1.75	Amblygonite	1.64	1.61
Kyanite	1.73	1.72	Topaz	1.63	1.62
Taaffeite	1.72	1.72	Nephrite	1.63	1.61
Idocrase	1.72	1.71	Hambergite	1.63	1.55
Sinhalite	1.71	1.67	Brazilianite	1.62	1.60
Zoisite	1.70	1.69	Beryl	1.59	1.57
Diopside	1.70	1.67	Scapolite	1.57	1.55
Olivine	1.69	1.65	Beryllonite	1.56	1.55
Axinite	1.69	1.68	Quartz	1.55	1.54
Kornerupine	1.68	1.67	Cordierite	1.55	1.54
Spodumene	1.68	1.66	Chalcedony	1.54	1.54
Phenakite	1.68	1.66	Orthoclase	1.53	1.52
Fibrolite	1.68	1.66			

Colour / dichroism and spectroscopic properties   With the exception of diamond, most precious stones like ruby, sapphire, emerald, spinel, etc., are prized because of their beautiful colours. The quality of colour is, however, an unreliable way of identifying cut stones, as a whole range of tints can be shown by specimens of the same species of gemstone, whilst specimens of different stones are often so similar in colour that it is only possible for the most expert eye to distinguish them.

Little is yet known of the substances which cause the tints in precious stones. This is due partly to the very small amounts in which they are present in the specimens, and the consequent difficulty in detecting them by chemical methods, and partly to the high cost of the material necessary for such analysis. In many precious stones the colour is due to chemical impurity and may be investigated by the use of the spectroscope. When white light is passed through a spectroscope, it is split into its constituent colours, red, orange, yellow, green, blue, indigo and violet. If certain chemical elements are made to emit light, for example by sparking in an electric arc or heating to white heat, bright lines can be seen superimposed on the ordinary spectrum. The position of these lines corresponds to dark bands which are seen when white light is passed through a transparent substance containing the same element and are known as absorption bands. If we examine with a spectroscope light which has passed through a gemstone, the position and number of the absorption bands will tell us what elements are present in the stone.

A good example of this use of the spectroscope is provided by the ruby. When analysed by ordinary chemical methods, ruby is found to consist of very nearly pure alumina. Spectroscopic examination, however, shows a number of narrow absorption bands in the deep red, a very broad absorption band in the green, and some narrow bands in the blue. These bands correspond to lines emitted by chromium when it is raised to a sufficiently high temperature, and are due to the presence of chromium in the ruby.

Many gemstones have characteristic absorption spectra and this not only frequently proves of considerable value in identifying them but also in distinguishing between them and their synthetic substitutes. Synthetic and natural blue spinel, for example, may easily be distinguished in this manner.

Another very convenient method of analysing the colour of stones is by means of a suitably chosen colour filter, such as the 'Chelsea' filter. This is a filter which only transmits a yellowish green and a deep red band of light. It is used primarily to distinguish between emerald and other green stones: emerald when illuminated by a strong light appears red when viewed through the filter whereas most of the other green stones remain green. The filter may also be used to distinguish synthetic blue spinel, which appears red, from other blue stones which do not change colour.

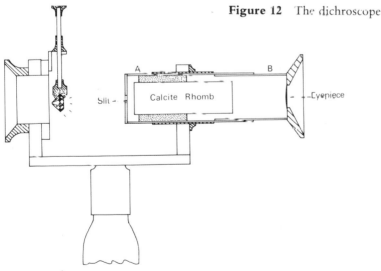

Figure 12   The dichroscope

Coloured doubly refracting stones sometimes show distinctly different colours according to the direction in which they are viewed. This phenomenon is called dichroism and is clearly seen in such a mineral as green tourmaline which appears almost black when viewed along the prism edge, whilst across the prism edge it appears light green. In many cases, however, the dichroism is so feeble that it cannot be observed by the naked eye, and an instrument called a dichroscope is then utilised. This, as shown in Figure 12, consists of a hollow tube A, in which is mounted a rhomb of calcite. One end of the tube is closed by a cap in which is cut a slit, whilst at the other end is inserted the tube B, carrying an eyepiece fitted with a lens, which can be focused on the slit by sliding the tube B in and out. Provision is made to mount the gemstone on a movable holder in front of the slit. Modern instruments can use polaroid.

On looking at the sky through the instrument we see two images of the slit owing to the double refraction of the calcite which splits the incident rays into two separate sets of rays. When a dichroic stone is placed in front of the slit, and either the instrument or the stone is rotated, the following facts may be observed. In four positions at 90° from each other, the images of the slit are identical in colour, but if the rotation from any such position is continued, a difference in colour can be noted which reaches a maximum at 45°; the difference then decreases until the next position at which identity of tint occurs is reached, and so on, until the rotation is completed. Thus in ruby, at the maximum difference the two images are coloured pale yellowish red and deep red respectively. On turning the stone the two images become increasingly similar until at 45° they are the same red colour. On turning further they change again until at 90° from the original position the first image has become deep red and the second image pale yellowish red.

Dichroism is due to double refraction and is never observed in singly refracting stones like garnet and spinel, nor in any coloured glass. Coloured doubly refracting stones are sometimes so feebly dichroic that no difference in the tints of the images can be observed, whilst dichroic stones do not exhibit the property if they are viewed along an optic axis. To eliminate errors arising from this latter fact one should always examine the stone in several directions. It is therefore clear that, whilst the presence of dichroism is a sure indication that the specimen is doubly refracting, absence of it does not imply that a stone is singly refracting.

Special optical appearances   Several stones, e.g. *moonstone, cat's-eye, labradorite*, and one or two others do not owe their beauty to the optical properties already described, but to the peculiar effects which are seen when light strikes their surface. These stones are usually translucent and are never faceted. They are cut either with a rounded surface, that is, *en cabochon*, or simply as flat polished plates.

The phenomenon adularescence is well shown in the moonstone (Case 15B), a variety of the potash–feldspar, adularia, from which the appearance is named. The crystal shows a tendency to part along certain crystallographic planes, resulting in the peculiar delicate play of light. The sheen is due to the reflection of light from numerous platy inclusions arranged parallel to these planes. There is a similar explanation for labradorite (Case 15A) and for the variety of chrysoberyl known as cat's-eye. The latter when cut *en cabochon*, often shows a broad band of white light which moves across the surface of the specimen as its position in relation to the observer is changed. This effect is known as chatoyancy and also appears in a variety of quartz known as *cat's-eye quartz* in this case due to the fibrous structure of the stone.

Asterism is shown by some sapphires and rubies—called, in consequence, *star-sapphires* and *star-rubies*—which exhibit a more or less well defined six-rayed star when cut *en cabochon* so that the greatest thickness of the specimen lies parallel to the vertical axis of the crystal. This appearance is caused by a series of microscopic canals lying in the crystal and arranged in directions which make

Table 4 Dichroic gemstones

Stone	Colour	Colours seen in dichroscope	
Andalusite	green or brown	green or yellowish green	brownish red
Axinite	brown	blue	brown or yellowish green
Benitoite	blue	pale blue	deep blue
Beryl: Aquamarine	bluish green	pale yellowish green	pale blue
Beryl: Emerald	green	yellowish green	bluish green
Chrysoberyl: Alexandrite	green	green	yellow to red
Corundum: Ruby	red	pale yellowish red	deep red
Corundum: Sapphire	blue	pale greenish blue	deep blue
Corundum: Sapphire	green	green	brown
Corundum: Sapphire	purple	almost colourless	violet
Cordierite	blue	yellowish grey	deep blue
Epidote	brown	yellowish green	deep brown
Euclase	pale green	pale green to colourless	green
Kyanite	blue	pale blue	dark blue
Quartz: Amethyst	purple	pale purple to yellow	deep purple
Quartz: Citrine★	yellow	pale yellow	yellow
Quartz: Smoky quartz	brown	pale yellow	yellowish brown
Sphene	brownish yellow	greenish yellow	reddish yellow
Sphene	green	deep green	reddish brown
Spodumene: Kunzite	pink	pale pink to colourless	purple to pink
Spodumene: Hiddenite	green	pale green	dark green
Topaz	yellow	pale pink or colourless	yellow
Topaz	pink	pale yellow or colourless	pinkish red
Topaz	blue	colourless	blue
Tourmaline	green	pale green	dark green
Tourmaline	red	pink	dark red
Tourmaline	blue	pale blue	dark blue
Tourmaline	brown	yellowish brown	deep brown
Zircon	blue	blue	pale blue to pale yellow
Zoisite	blue	purple/blue	sage green

★ Only natural stones show this dichroism: heat-treated stones show practically none.

angles of 60° with one another.

Sometimes internal flaws cause a play of prismatic colours, and a good example of this is shown by a specimen of rock crystal in Case 8B. The colours in such cases result from the interference of light which is occasioned by the thin film within the specimen.

Thermal and electrical properties

Precious stones conduct heat well and always feel much colder than imitations in glass. By simply touching a specimen with the tip of the tongue, it is possible after a little practice, to distinguish readily between paste and a genuine stone. If the specimen is small it is best to hold it in a pair of pincers, as it may get so heated up that the test can no longer be applied if held in the hand.

Most gemstones when rubbed with a material like flannel acquire an electrical charge and retain it for longer or shorter periods. Before the discovery of many of the interesting optical properties already described, electrical properties were sometimes used to discriminate between stones, but little use is made of them now.

Some minerals acquire an electrical charge on heating, and in consequence are called pyro-electric. This property is clearly exhibited by *tourmaline* and *topaz*.

Chemical properties

The simple substances or elements, which enter into the composition of gem-stones are usually of the commonest description. Thus, the metal aluminium, which is one of the most widely distributed elements in the earth's crust, is found in the majority of precious stones. Combined with oxygen alone, it forms the *ruby* and the *sapphire*, and it is an essential constituent in many of the silicates, e.g. *topaz, tourmaline, beryl* (including *emerald*), several of the *garnets*, etc., which are used for ornamental purposes. In the *spinel*, oxide of aluminium is united to that of magnesium, whilst in the *chrysoberyl* it is combined with the oxide of beryllium which is a much rarer element. *Turquoise* consists largely of aluminium phosphate and is the only gemstone of importance which contains the element phosphorus.

Silicon is the most widely distributed of all the elements of the earth's crust, with the exception of oxygen, and occurs as a constituent of many gemstones. In combination with oxygen, as silicon dioxide, or *silica*, it forms *rock crystal, cairngorm, amethyst, chalcedony*, and *agate*, and it is present as an essential consti-tuent in the silicates mentioned above.

Diamond, unique in many respects amongst precious stones, is composed of pure carbon, and is the only stone consisting of a single element. *Tourmaline*, on the other hand, may be cited as an example of complex composition containing many elements.

Although chemical analysis is a certain method of identifying a specimen, modern methods, for example X-ray diffraction, can be carried out without damaging the specimen. Such operations are rarely necessary as the identity of a stone can definitely be established by means of the physical tests already de-scribed.

3 CUTTING OF GEMSTONES

Precious stones as they occur in nature do not display prominently any of the beautiful qualities which have been referred to in the previous chapter. Some of them, it is true, are found in well-formed crystals with the faces showing a good lustre, but many of them occur in the sands and gravels of rivers as water-worn pebbles, which present by no means the attractive appearance popularly associated with this class of minerals. Even when, as in the case of the emerald, the stone is normally found as crystals in the mother-rock, it rarely happens that a specimen shows sufficient freedom from internal and external blemishes to warrant its being mounted without further treatment.

Transparent stones are usually cut with plane faces, or *facets*, whilst translucent or opaque stones, especially those showing any of the special optical effects mentioned in the last chapter, are cut *en cabochon*, i.e. with a rounded surface. According to the arrangement of the facets there are four main styles of cutting, known respectively as the Brilliant, the Step or Trap Cut, the Mixed Cut, and the Rose or Rosette.

The Brilliant Figure 13a, b and c represents a stone cut in this manner. The greatest circumference, or *girdle*, divides the specimen into an upper part, or *crown*, and a lower part, the *pavilion* or *culasse*. In the crown (Figure 13a) there are 33 facets made up as follows:

Table (A)	1
Star facets (B)	8
Templets or bezels (C)	4
Quoins or lozenges (D)	4
Cross facets or Skew facets (E)	8
Skill facets (F)	8
Total	33

It is common practice to consider the templets and quoins together as eight templets and the cross and skill facets together as sixteen cross facets.

Culet (G)	1
Pavilion facets (H)	4
Quoins (K)	4
Cross facets (L)	8
Skill facets (M)	8
Total	25

Figure 13   The brilliant: a upper part or crown; b view of side; c lower part or pavilion

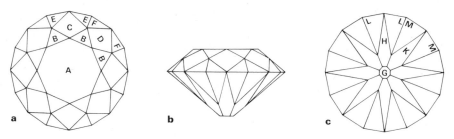

Here again it is more common to consider the pavilions and quoins together as eight pavilions and the cross and skill facets as sixteen cross facets.

This form of cutting is by far the most important, as it is used on all the best diamonds and on many other stones, both coloured and colourless. In the case of diamond there is a certain proportion about the finished brilliant which gives the maximum of 'fire' and 'life'. Of the total thickness of the stone, i.e. the distance between the table and the culet, one-third should be occupied by the crown, and two-thirds by the pavilion, whilst the diameter of the table should be about half that of the girdle and the culet one fifth that of the table.

The Step or Trap   Figure 14a, b and c represent a stone cut in this manner. In the upper part there is a table with a series of rows of facets sloping down towards the girdle, whilst in the under part the rows of facets slope away from the girdle to the culet. There is considerable variation in the number of rows of facets, and also in the outline of the girdle, which may be square, eight-sided, as in the illustration, or six-sided.

This style of cutting is often used in the treatment of coloured stones, and is usually preferred in the case of emerald.

Figure 14   The step cut: a upper part; b view of side; c lower part

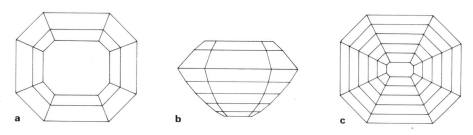

The Mixed Cut   In this form of cutting the specimen is made with the upper part as a brilliant and the lower part cut in steps. It possesses some of the advantages of having much of the fire of a brilliant while, since the depth of the base is not fixed, the stone may be cut deeper or shallower to produce the most pleasing colour effects.

The Rose Cut   The upper part of a stone cut in this way is shown in Figure 15a, and the side view in Figure 15b. It consists of six low triangular facets A, from the base of which the six triangular facets B slope down to the girdle. The spaces between the facets B are occupied by twelve facets C, which meet the girdle in an edge. There are thus in this part of the stone twenty-four facets, which are divided into the six star facets A, known as the *crown*, and eighteen cross facets B

Figure 15 The rose cut: a upper part; b view of side

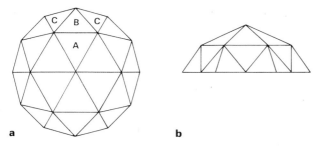

a   b

and c, called the *dentelle*. The under part of the stone usually consists of a broad flat face, which in the case of the diamond is usually a cleavage plane. Sometimes the under part is simply a repetition of the upper, which is called a *double rose*.

There are several types of rose in which the number of facets may be greater or smaller, but this one is most widely used.

In addition to these basic forms of cutting there is a large variety of other styles which are mainly modified brilliants. Cuts of less symmetrical outline include the *briolette*, the *marquise* and the *pendeloque* (Figures 16, 17, 18).

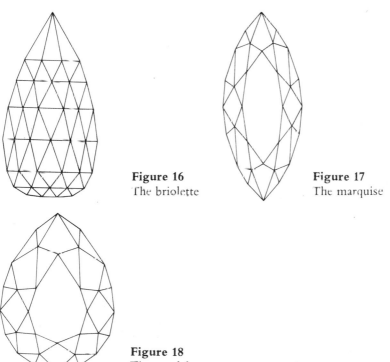

Figure 16
The briolette

Figure 17
The marquise

Figure 18
The pendeloque

The rounded forms call for little explanation. As mentioned above, they are usually employed for translucent and opaque stones, although transparent stones, especially garnets, are sometimes treated in this way. The *simple cabochon* (Figure 19) has a flat base, which may be oval or circular, whilst in the *double cabochon* the under part also consists of a dome, which is, however, usually flatter than that of the upper part (Figure 20).

In the *hollowed cabochon* (Figure 21) the interior of the stone has been ground away, thus giving it a shell-like form; several of the garnets shown in Case 17B have been treated in this way, and as a result their transparency greatly increased.

Figure 19
Simple cabochon

Figure 20
Double cabochon

Figure 21
Hollow cabochon

The actual process of cutting is carried out on a metal disc which is provided with the powder of some hard substance to act as grinding material. The metal disc—about one foot in diameter—is mounted on a vertical axis and rotates horizontally at a high velocity. The metal varies with the hardness of the stone to be treated and it may consist of iron, brass, copper, tin, or lead.

The grinding material also varies according to the stone which is being cut. Diamond is the hardest of all substances and can only be abraded by its own powder. Samples of diamond powder are shown in the abrasives bay on the second gallery of the Museum. Stones like ruby and sapphire are also cut with diamond powder which, despite its high cost, is employed because it allows the work to be done quickly.

Powdered *emery*, a natural mixture of corundum and magnetite, is extensively used for the softer stones and, in recent years, the artificial abrasive *carborundum*, a carbide of silicon, which is harder than corundum, has also been used.

The abrasive is made into a paste with olive oil or water and spread on the outer part of the disc into which it gradually works its way, providing a circular file which cuts out the facet. After the stone has been given the required shape it has to be polished, and this is usually achieved on a disc of softer material with some such polishing agent as tripoli (a form of silica), putty powder (a mixture of tin and lead oxides), rouge (iron oxide), etc., applied to the wheel in a paste.

Diamond, on account of its great hardness, is treated in a different way from any other stone. If its natural shape is not suitable for the style of cutting chosen, advantage is taken of the cleavage to remove superfluous material. The diamond splitter mounts the stone in cement at the end of a rod and makes an incision in the proper direction with another diamond similarly mounted. He then inserts a chisel into the cut, gives it a smart tap with a hammer and splits off the unnecessary portion. This is repeated until the stone is in the desired shape and ready for *bruting*. The stone is mounted in cement and rubbed against another diamond in the same way, and the stone is roughly shaped. This process used to be carried out by hand but now the stone to be cut is mounted in a special metal holder, called a *dop*, held in the chuck of a mechanically driven lathe. The second diamond, mounted in a similar dop fixed to the end of a long rod, is then pressed against the rapidly revolving stone.

When the stone has been roughly shaped the facets are ground and polished on an iron wheel, revolving at high speed and covered with a paste of olive oil and diamond powder.

The manner in which the diamond is held in its holder is interesting. The holder, or drop, consists of a copper cup, attached to a small rod, and filled with a fusible solder of lead and tin alloy. The stone is embedded in this with the part to be ground left exposed. Mechanical dops, in which the diamond is held by steel claws, are also used.

The dop is clamped by the small rod to a horizontal bar positioned so that the cup hangs downward with the stone resting on the polishing wheel. As many as four stones are polished at the same time on one wheel, the pressure on each being varied by lead weights placed on the horizontal bars.

The nature of the surface of polished stones depends upon the type of gemstone. In all stones except diamond the friction of polishing causes an extremely thin fused surface layer, known as the *Beilby layer*. In diamond the melting point is too high for surface fusion to take place and the process of polishing is here only a matter of wearing the stone successively smoother. In some of the other gemstones the Beilby layer remains as an amorphous skin whilst in others it recrystallises immediately after its formation.

4 IMITATION, TREATMENT, AND ARTIFICIAL FORMATION OF GEMSTONES

The more valuable gemstones have been much admired from the earliest times, and it is not surprising that imitations have been made with great ingenuity resembling the natural product at least in outward appearance. Glass is an obvious choice for this purpose as glassmaking is a very old industry and counterfeits were well known to our ancestors who acquired considerable skill in manufacturing them.

It sometimes happens that very slight differences in the tints of specimens of the same stone make very considerable differences in value and various devices have been to treat the less valuable variety so that it may resemble the more costly one for a time at least. These deceptions may be intended only for the purchaser, but some are well recognised processes of treatment for permanently altering the appearance of a stone. A few typical instances will be given here and others will be referred to when the particular gems are described.

Until the last few decades all the collector had to fear was the glass imitation mentioned above, but at the beginning of the century *corundum*, including its varieties *ruby* and *sapphire*, was successfully manufactured, the stones cut from this artificial material being identical with the natural ones in optical and other physical properties. Careful examination under the microscope is the only satisfactory method of distinguishing the natural from the manufactured ruby and, as the difference in value is enormous, the advent of this artificial product caused considerable anxiety in the precious stone trade.

Keeping these facts in mind, the collector will do well to buy specimens unmounted whenever possible. When a stone is mounted, flaws are easily hidden, devices for improving its appearance are difficult to detect, several diagnostic physical properties cannot be determined, and microscopic examination is difficult.

Imitation of precious stones

Various kinds of glass are used for this purpose, referred to commercially as *paste* or *strass* the latter being better quality imitations. When counterfeiting ruby, sapphire, emerald, topaz etc. the colour is obtained by the addition of small quantities of suitable metallic oxides. The glass used for imitating such a stone as diamond must possess a high refractive index, a high lustre, and strong dispersive power, qualities which are attained by the addition of lead, and, less commonly, thallium. The use of such ingredients, however, not only diminishes the hardness of the product but also renders it liable to alteration and, consequently, after some time it becomes cloudy and loses much of its initial brilliancy.

The making of a good paste is no simple matter. The ingredients must be of extreme purity to avoid accidental colouring, whilst the cooling of the molten material must be carried out slowly and carefully in order to produce a transparent mass free from air-bubbles and striae. The constituents are usually pure quartz, carbonate or nitrate of potash, and red lead, the proportions of these vary depending on the intended use of the paste. The substances are powdered, mixed, and, with the addition of a little borax, fused in a crucible. The mass is then allowed to cool very slowly, after which the clear transparent product is ready for cutting. Such a glass is colourless, but, by the addition of very small proportions of various metallic oxides, it can be made to assume any tint. A blue colour is produced by cobalt oxide, red by cuprous oxide, ruby-red by the addition of some gold compound such as purple of Cassius, green by either cupric or chromic oxide, violet by manganese oxide and so on.

Reference has already been made to the fact that glass is warmer to the touch than a natural stone, and the test mentioned on p. 17 is usually quite sufficient for anyone who has had any practice in this kind of work. A paste imitation yields to the file whilst a genuine stone does not, but this is a drastic method of testing, and if it is necessary to use it, the scratch should be made in an inconspicuous place, for example on the girdle, the stone being examined with a lens. For more satisfactory confirmation that the specimen is of glass the stone should be examined to see if it is singly refracting, and bubbles and striae should be searched for with a microscope.

A cut specimen may sometimes be made with an upper part, or crown, of genuine stone, whilst the lower part, or pavilion, consists of inferior material. Such devices are known as *doublets*, of which several varieties exist. The doublet may consist of two pieces of natural stone cemented together, or the upper part may be of a valuable stone like diamond, whilst the lower part consists of a cheaper stone like white corundum.

In the *triplet* a layer of coloured glass or cement impregnated with a deeply coloured dye is inserted between two pieces of genuine material.

The doublet and triplet are difficult to detect when mounted, but tests of an unset specimen show that all the physical properties do not usually agree with those of any natural stone, whilst if the specimen is immersed in hot water or an organic solvent, the cement softens and the parts separate.

Artificial treatment of precious stones

One of the most valuable kinds of diamond is known as the 'blue-white', which is very rare as the majority of stones possess a yellowish tinge, quite visible to the practised eye. When blue wax or varnish is rubbed over the back of a yellow stone the tint is 'corrected' and the specimen appears quite white. The device is only temporary, as the colouring matter is bound to go sooner or later and the true colour then makes its appearance. The trick can always be detected by washing the stone in alcohol and so dissolving off the pigment.

Many stones alter their colour when heated and this fact is used in the case of topaz, zircon, and quartz.

At present the most valuable kind of topaz possesses a pink colour but such stones are rare. The yellow topaz is, however, readily changed to pink by heating, and the great majority of pink stones on the market today have been produced in this way. The topaz is packed in a crucible with some inert material such as magnesia and heated carefully. If the stone is of Brazilian origin it turns white and on cooling assumes the beautiful pink colour shown by some of the specimens in Case 3B. Stones from other localities do not change to this colour.

Some kinds of zircon when heated not only become colourless but also show a considerable increase in lustre. The refractive index of this stone is high, and colourless zircons obtained by 'burning' have frequently been passed off as diamonds. The fraud may be readily detected owing to the strong double refraction of zircon. If an edge of one of the back facets is examined through the table facet with a lens, it will be seen doubly, a convincing proof of the double refraction of the stone.

By varying the conditions of heating, zircons can also be made to acquire a delicate blue or a golden-yellow colour.

The dark variety of quartz, known as *morion*, becomes colourless at high temperatures. At a moderate temperature the colour changes from almost black to a rich brown, and in this form the material is frequently sold as 'Spanish topaz'. The dichroism shown by heat-treated quartz is considerably less intense than that shown by naturally coloured stones.

The colourless variety of quartz is sometimes treated in a peculiar manner. The stone is heated to a fairly high temperature and then plunged into a solution of dye, numerous cracks are developed, and the dye soaks along them. These stones can be detected at a glance as the colouring is not uniform but is confined to the fissures produced by the sudden cooling.

Examples of the above methods of artificial treatment will be found in the cases devoted to the minerals mentioned and other instances of staining and colouring will be referred to when the particular stones are described. Some stones change colour after irradiation in an atomic pile or by X-rays.

Artificial formation of precious stones

It has already been pointed out how unsatisfactory the glass imitation is compared with the natural stone, and how easily it can be detected. With the advance in the knowledge of the composition of minerals chemists began to direct their attention towards producing them in the laboratory. Predictably much ingenious work was carried out on precious stones to produce a substance comparable with the natural one.

The only stones which, up till now, have been successfully manufactured are *corundum* (including *ruby* and *sapphire*), *spinel* and, in recent years, *emerald*, the beautiful green variety of beryl. Diamonds have been formed up to a carat size of gem quality but are more expensive than the natural stones.

Corundum consists of crystallised oxide of aluminium, or alumina, and includes several varieties which have different names depending on their colour: thus, *ruby* is transparent red corundum and *sapphire* is transparent blue corundum.

As usually prepared in the laboratory, alumina is a white amorphous powder and the problem of converting this material into transparent crystallised corundum or, alternatively, of forming it under conditions in which it would assume the crystallised state remained unsolved for a considerable time. The early attempts, commenced in 1837, were unsuccessful, but in 1877 thin, platy crystals of ruby were produced by Frémy and Feil. Later, Frémy and Verneuil produced rubies large enough to be cut in rose form, but they were too small for general use in jewellery.

About the year 1885, a number of very perfect rubies appeared on the market in Geneva. They possessed all the characters of the natural mineral, but were seen to contain a number of rounded air-bubbles. They were sold at a high price and the secret of their manufacture was well kept, but it seems to be practically certain that they were made by fusing up a number of smaller rubies in the oxyhydrogen blowpipe and letting the mass so obtained cool and crystallise out. This process was known as *reconstruction* and was applied with some success in 1895, and during the succeeding years.

Nowadays artificial rubies are not reconstructed from fragments of the natural stone, but are made from pure alumina, prepared from ammonium alum, to which oxide of chromium is added to produce the red colour. Commercially the material is prepared by calcining ammonium alum, double sulphate of ammonium and aluminium, to which a little chromium has been added usually in the form of chromic sulphate. After treatment the alumina forms a freely flowing powder containing about 1.3 per cent chromic oxide. The mixture is fused by a blowpipe fed with hydrogen and oxygen, and, with certain precautions, a clear transparent mass of ruby is obtained. It had been known for a long time that alumina could be fused by an oxygen blowpipe, but all attempts to produce a large transparent mass had failed until Verneuil took the problem up, and succeeded in reaching a solution in a series of brilliant researches. The following is a short account of his results which were published in 1904.

He found that, to obtain a clear transparent product from the fusion of alumina, these three conditions had to be observed:

1   The fusion must be carried out in that part of the flame which, whilst capable of melting alumina, is richest in hydrogen in order to avoid bubbles.
2   The mass must grow upwards in regular superposed layers.
3   The cooling surface, i.e. the contact of the fused mass with the support, must be as small as possible.

Verneuil designed a most ingenious piece of apparatus embodying these principles and was able to produce large transparent masses of ruby with it.

The modern form of the apparatus is very similar to his and is shown in Figure 22.

It consists essentially of a vertical oxy-hydrogen blowpipe, the upper part is in the form of a fairly large chamber c extended downwards by a tube т ending in the jet J. Hydrogen is fed by tube н into the outer casing surrounding the tube. The sieve A, containing the finely powdered mixture of alumina and chromic oxide is suspended by a peg held in a flexible diaphragm. The oxygen enters the blowpipe by an opening o in the upper chamber. The peg is tapped by a mechanically operated hammer every two or three seconds, so that the powder is shaken out of the sieve and is carried along to the flame in the current of oxygen. The refractory support R on which the molten mass grows may be lowered, usually by hand, by means of a simple gearing device. The refractory cylindrical bricks в form a guard around the jet.

The first particles of powder which fall upon the refractory support R form a conical mass of sintered material which gradually grows upwards until the apex reaches a part of the flame sufficiently hot to liquefy the alumina and the powder which arrives thereafter melts and forms a fine thread. As this spread grows upwards it gradually reaches a hotter region of the flame and a little sphere is formed on the summit. The support is then lowered a little and the temperature of the flame increased so that the top of the molten mass increases in size. Eventually a pear-shaped mass or *boule* of ruby results. The remarkable thing about these *boules* is that, although possessing no crystal faces, yet they have the internal crystalline structure of the natural ruby and are identical with it in hardness, specific gravity, refractive index, double refraction and dichroism. The structure of the boule is that of a single crystal which is not set in any particular orientation in relation to its shape. If, however, by suitably controlling the conditions, a long thin rod is grown instead of a stout boule, the vertical (optic) axis of the crystal, starting in any position in the early formed parts of the rod, gradually turns over until eventually it is perpendicular to the length of the rod.

When the boule has grown and been allowed to cool, a blow on the stem usually splits it into two roughly symmetrical halves, along a plane which contains the optic axis. Commercially boules are grown up to about 300 carats and are largely used for 'jewels' for the bearings of watches, electrical instruments and lasers.

Figure 22   Inverted blowpipe apparatus

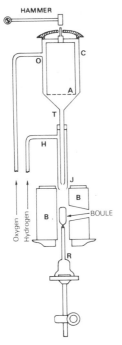

The production of sapphire proved a more difficult problem. Oxide of cobalt was added to the pure alumina, but all attempts to get a clear, transparent mass with the characteristic blue colour failed. It was found that by adding some magnesia to the mixture a transparent, blue flux resulted and this was cut and put on the market as 'Hope sapphire'. On examination, however, these stones proved by their hardness, specific gravity, absence of dichroism, etc., to be *spinel*. Examples of them are shown in the case.

By adding small quantities of iron and titanium oxides to the alumina, Verneuil at last succeeded in preparing a clear transparent, blue product answering in all respects to the natural sapphire; examples of these are shown.

The green stones are produced by the addition of vanadium. They possess the interesting property of appearing red by lamp-light and have been wrongly called 'reconstructed alexandrites.' The pale pink stone is, in like manner, often wrongly designated 'reconstructed' or 'scientific topaz', whilst the colourless artificial corundum has sometimes been sold quite falsely as 'synthetic diamond'. The yellow colour seen in some of the *boules* is obtained by adding 3 per cent of nickel oxide to the alumina; these stones also have incorrectly been called 'scientific topaz'. Star stones are now made by the addition of extra titania.

It will be seen from the above remarks that none of the tests mentioned in Chapter 2 serves to distinguish the artificial from the natural corundum. As at present manufactured the former usually shows rounded air-bubbles and curved striae which can sometimes be seen with a lens, but are often visible only under the microscope. Detection of synthetic stones is most readily carried out when the stone, immersed in a cell filled with a liquid of similar refractive index, is examined under a binocular microscope and the characteristic flaws referred to above observed. Natural rubies also show striae and cavities but the former are straight lines whilst the latter have not a rounded bubble-shape but have definite crystal-outlines.

In contrast to the success achieved in the artificial production of the ruby, all the efforts made to produce the *diamond* on a form fit for jewellery have so far proved too expensive.

Diamond consists of pure carbon crystallised in the cubic system and the pressure and temperature necessary to convert the black amorphous carbon, or charcoal, into the beautiful crystallised variety are so difficult to achieve in the laboratory that, after many attempts the only result has been a few microscopic, badly-formed crystals which are utterly unfit for any of the purposes to which the diamond is applied.

Attempts to synthesise diamond have been made, but until recently only the results of J. B. Hannay, a Glasgow chemist, had been accepted. His method depended on the fact that when a gas containing hydrogen and carbon is heated with a metal such as sodium, potassium or lithium, the hydrogen combines with the metal, setting free the carbon. Accordingly he took a mixture of lithium, bone oil, and paraffin, sealed it up in a stout iron tube and heated it for several hours in a furnace. The lithium united with the hydrogen of the hydro-carbons and liberated the carbon under great pressure. The tube, after being allowed to cool, was opened and found to contain a hard black mass in which were embedded minute crystals having all the properties of diamond. These experiments were carried out in 1880 and of eighty attempts only three were successful; the rest failed owing usually to the bursting of the tube under the enormous pressure, or to leakage through the tube which became porous at red heat. The largest specimen of diamond produced was only a small fraction of an inch across. Recent work suggests that Hannay's diamonds are natural but that the starting materials may have been contaminated by diamond fragments.

Among other methods which have been tried may be mentioned that used in 1893 by Moissan who dissolved carbon in iron in an electric furnace and then rapidly cooled the molten mass by plunging it into water; and that of Friedländer, who stirred fused olivine with a rod of graphite. Although these and other workers may have been successful in producing diamond, their results were not confirmed. In 1954, the synthesis of diamond was achieved in the research laboratories of the General Electric Company of America. The largest crystal then produced had a length of 1.2 millimetres. The process has now been developed commercially, for industrial diamond, in the U.S.A., South Africa and elsewhere, and millions of carats are prepared annually. The stones are mainly less than $\frac{1}{16}$th mm across.

Synthetic *emeralds* have been made hydrothermally by Nacken and Linde and by the flux melt process of Zerfass, Germany, Chatham, U.S.A. and Gilson, France. They contain veil-like inclusions and the constants are somewhat lower than those of the natural stones; examples are shown in Case 5A.

Rutile (titanium dioxide) has been produced synthetically since World War II. The dispersion is several times greater than that of diamond, and the cut stones show an extraordinary 'fire'.

Other man-made materials used to simulate diamond are *GGG* (*Gadolinium gallium 'garnet'*), *lithium niobate, strontium titanate* and *YAG* (*Yttrium aluminium 'garnet'*) but pride of place goes to *cubic zirconia*; this is the most difficult to distinguish from the natural stones.

More recently Gilson in France has produced synthetic black and white precious *opal, lapis-lazuli* and *turquoise*. Examples may be seen in the appropriate cases.

Table 5   Man-made diamond simulants

Material	Specific gravity	Hardness	Refraction	Refractive Indices
GGG	7.05	6	single	2.03
Synthetic scheelite	6.1–5.9	$4\frac{1}{2}$	double	1.94–1.92
Cubic zirconia	5.7	$8\frac{1}{2}$	single	2.18
Strontium titanate	5.13	6	single	2.41
Lithium niobate	4.64	6	double	2.30–2.21
YAG	4.57	$8\frac{1}{2}$	single	1.83
Synthetic rutile	4.25	$6\frac{1}{2}$	double	2.90–2.62

5 DESCRIPTION OF GEMSTONES CONTAINED IN THE COLLECTION

In this Chapter the minerals are described; a plan of the arrangement of the gemstone cases is shown in Figure 1.

Diamond (CASES 1A and 2A)

Hardness, 10; Specific gravity, 3.52; Singly refracting; Refractive index, 2.42.

In many respects diamond occupies a unique position amongst precious stones. It is commonly regarded as the gemstone *par excellence* and is the one most generally employed by jewellers. To the mineralogist it appeals strongly on account of its many unique properties; it is the hardest known substance; it consists of a single element; it is combustible; its refraction and dispersion are extraordinarily strong; its crystals are usually complex and have many of the faces rounded in a curious manner. Finally, in the commercial world, diamond is the most important gemstone, for more capital is invested in its exploitation than in any other member of the series.

Two Florentine academicians showed, in 1695, that diamond disappeared when sunlight was focused upon it through a powerful lens, and its chemical identity with pure carbon was proved by Smithson Tennant a century later. It is possible to convert diamond into graphite by subjecting it to a high temperature and excluding air.

The crystals of diamond belong to the cubic system, and the faces, as already mentioned, are frequently rounded. The common forms are the octahedron (Figure 23) and the dodecahedron (Figure 24) whilst crystals of cubical form (Figure 25) are rarer. The octahedral planes are sometimes replaced by three or six-faced pyramids, thus giving rise to triakis-octahedral and hexakis-octahedral forms. A set of models illustrating these and other more complicated forms is exhibited.

Another point of interest exhibited by the octahedral crystals from South Africa is that the edges of the octahedron are replaced by striated grooves which show that what appears to be a simple crystal is in reality a compound or twin form (Figure 23).

Diamond cleaves very readily parallel to the octahedral planes which makes it brittle and easily reduced to powder. The extraordinary hardness of the diamond has often been confused with the quality of toughness or tenacity, i.e. the power of resisting a blow, an old way of 'testing' a doubtful specimen consisted in laying it on an anvil and striking it with a hammer. If the stone broke, then it was pronounced a fake. Needless to say, many diamonds failed to resist such treatment.

Absolutely colourless diamond, i.e. 'fine-white' stones, or diamonds 'of the first water', are rather uncommon and are highly prized. Faint tinges of yellow, green, and brown frequently occur and are shown by several of the specimens in the case; a black diamond from Brazil is also exhibited. Various shades of yellow are characteristic of the Cape diamonds, but the colour is often so faint that it can be detected only by placing the stone side by side with a colourless one. Deeply coloured diamonds are rare and, when flawless, command very high prices. The colour of diamonds is very stable and is influenced but slightly by heat or by radium rays. When diamond is exposed to the action of radioactivity in a dark room it becomes phosphorescent. In this respect, the only other gemstone which it resembles is kunzite (p. 54).

Figure 23 Octahedral crystal of diamond   **Figure 24** Dodecahedral crystal of diamond   **Figure 25** Cubic crystal of diamond

    Stones which superficially resemble diamond include white sapphire, topaz, zircon and rock crystal; synthetic spinel, synthetic rutile, synthetic scheelite, lithium niobate, strontium titanate, Y.A.G., G.G.G., cubic zirconia and paste (glass). The hardness and superb surface lustre—so characteristic that its description, *adamantine*, comes from the Greek word αδαμας *adamas*, from which *diamond* is derived—serve to distinguish the diamond from all other stones. Diamond (hardness 10) scratches corundum easily and a very ready means of testing a doubtful specimen is to try its effect on a polished plate of that mineral.

    The styles in which diamond is cut have already been described (pp. 19–21).

    Specimens of cut diamonds are shown here, in a central case near the large Siberian Aventurine vase and a beautiful gold snuff-box set with sixteen large brilliant-cut stones and numerous other small ones can be seen. Both the snuff-box and the vase were presented by Nicholas I, Emperor of Russia, to Sir Roderick Murchison, who bequeathed them to the Museum.

    On the removal of the Museum from Jermyn Street to South Kensington the snuff-box and vase passed by the terms of the bequest to the Mineral Department, British Museum, but at the request of the Trustees of the British Museum, and with the assent of the Trustees of Sir Roderick Murchison, they are allowed to remain on loan to the Geological Museum.

    The most productive localities for gem diamonds are South Africa, U.S.S.R., Namibia and Zaire. Angola, Ghana, Sierra Leone, Botswana, Tanzania, Ivory Coast, Brazil and Venezuela are also important producers, whilst India was the only source until diamonds were discovered in Brazil in 1725.

    The mines in *India* were at one time very productive and the prejudice in favour of Indian diamonds was so strong that, on the discovery of the Brazilian deposits in 1725, the stones were sent to India and exported from there as Indian diamonds. India is now unimportant as a diamond-producer.

    The diamond-bearing deposits are confined to the eastern slope of the Deccan and are found scattered over the area extending from the Penner River in the south almost to the Ganges in the north. The mines occur in groups of which those situated 200 miles east of the fortress of Golconda—hence known as the Golconda Mines—are the most famous. The diamonds occurred in loose alluvium lying close to the banks of the Kistna River. From this locality came the famous 'Koh-i-Noor', and the 'Hope Blue'.

Samples of the diamond-bearing alluvium from Cuddapah, on the Penner River, are shown here. A group of mines was situated in this neighbourhood and west of it at Wajra Karur a pipe of blue rock similar to the famous *blue ground* of the Kimberley mines was discovered but unfortunately it carried no diamonds.

In *Brazil* diamonds are found over a wide area, the two most productive states being Minas Gerais and Bahia. The stones occur in a deposit known as *cascalho* which has resulted from the disintegration of itacolumite, a laminated micaceous sandstone characteristic of the region. The richest mines in Minas Gerais are situated in the Diamantina district, whilst in Bahia the Sincuramines have been very productive. It is from the latter locality that the valuable *carbonado* is obtained. It occurs in nodules and consists of an aggregate of small crystals of diamond mixed with various impurities. It has no cleavage and, on account of its extraordinary hardness, is in great demand for mounting the crowns of rock-drills. Specimens of carbonado are shown here.

South Africa far outstrips in importance any other region hitherto discovered. Here the deposits are of extraordinary richness and, so far, appear to be inexhaustible. The majority of them are worked by the powerful De Beers Company, who have applied the most approved methods of mining and winning the diamonds and exercise a large controlling influence in the diamond market of the world.

There are two sources of the diamond in South Africa, known respectively as the river diggings and the dry diggings. The former are situated for the most part in the valley of the Vaal River, where the diamonds are found in the gravels of the river-bed and in the adjacent alluvial terraces. The material, as seen in the specimens shown here, consists largely of siliceous pebbles. It is excavated, washed and passed through a sieve and the diamonds are picked out by hand from the concentrate They are of superior quality and fetch more per carat than the produce of the dry diggings.

The dry diggings were discovered in 1870 and have proved the richest source of diamond in the world. The first deposits were found at Jagersfontein, in the Orange River State, and, shortly afterwards, the mines in the neighbourhood of what is now the town of Kimberley were discovered. Since that time new finds have been made at various other places and, in 1902, an exceedingly rich mine—The Premier Mine—was found near Pretoria.

In character all the mines are similar. The deposits fill vertical pipes which pierce shales, quartzite and igneous rock and extend downwards to an unknown depth. The pipes have a diameter at the surface varying from 200 to 700 yards and sometimes the sides tend to converge as greater depths are reached. The material filling them consists of a soft but tenacious blue rock known as *blue ground* which is soapy to the touch and which alters at the surface to a yellow friable earth, the *yellow ground* of the miners. Samples of these carrying diamonds are shown in the case.

The *blue ground* consists essentially of a finely divided serpentinous matrix in which are embedded boulders and angular fragments of rock together with such minerals as olivine, often altered to serpentine, ruby-red garnet ('Cape ruby'), diopside, ilmenite, enstatite, mica, tourmaline, etc.

The diamonds are confined to the blue ground and are never found in the surrounding rocks—known as reef—which abut sharply on the pipes. They vary in size from large stones of 100 carats and over down to the smallest ones which are almost invisible to the naked eye.

'Fine-white' stones occur, but many of the South African crystals exhibit a more or less pronounced yellow tinge, whilst others are distinctly brown. The concentration of the diamonds in the matrix is extremely small, varying from 0.23 carats to 0.38 carats per load of 16 cubic feet, and the richness of the deposits arises from the inexhaustible supply of blue ground which is available.

The generally accepted view regarding the pipes is that they represent sites of ancient volcanic activity and that the blue ground was formed by the shattering of a deep-seated igneous magma rich in olivine. The pipes or necks were produced by a series of explosions which pulverised the magma and forced it into the vents where it became mixed with fragments of the surrounding rocks. The diamonds probably existed in the original olivine rock where they had crystallised out under suitable conditions of temperature and pressure when the rock was fluid. Subsequently the rock experienced the volcanic forces which shattered it. The fact that many of the crystals are broken and show distinct signs of having been subjected to rough usage support this theory.

Since its formation, the breccia of the pipes has been weathered and altered; the olivine has been converted largely into serpentine, and a considerable amount of carbonate of lime has been formed as well as various zeolites.

Mining of the blue ground is carried on from shafts sunk in the surrounding rock. Tunnels are driven from these to the pipes and the diamond-bearing material is excavated layer by layer. Formerly the blue ground was spread in fields for several months to facilitate decomposition and disintegration, but it is now sieved at the mine-head, and the larger pieces crushed by special rollers which do not damage the diamonds. The crushed ore is then conveyed to the washing machines which separate the lighter material and leave a residue consisting of garnet, ilmenite, pyrite, etc., with the diamonds. A sample of this is shown.

Formerly the diamonds were picked out by hand, but a highly interesting mechanical process is now used. It depends on the fact that diamond, unlike most minerals, has a greater affinity for grease than for water. The residue is passed over inclined plates covered with grease and the diamonds cling to these whilst the other minerals pass on causing a complete separation.

Zaire is the most important source of diamonds in the world from the point of view of weight. Three-quarters of the world's bort, cryptocrystalline diamond unsuitable for gemstones and used as a cutting, abrading and polishing medium, is produced by Zaire. The diamonds occur in gravels, where they are associated with many other heavy minerals. The fields extend into the neighbouring territory of *Angola,* itself an important diamond-producing country.

In *Ghana,* diamonds, worked principally for industrial use are found associated with staurolite, ilmenite and other minerals in river gravels.

Since the discovery in 1930 of diamonds in river gravels in *Sierra Leone,* this country has become an important producer, and, in recent years, has yielded some very large stones. In 1947 a stone weighing 770 carats was discovered and one of 968.9 carats, the third largest stone ever to be found, was discovered in 1972.

Namibia is another important source of diamonds which occur in a superficial deposit of coarse sand with rounded and wind-faceted pebbles of quartz, jasper, agate, garnet, epidote, etc. This deposit is confined to the coastal belt and diamonds have been found in it over a region stretching southwards some 500 miles from Walvis Bay and probably forms the richest single source of gem diamonds in the world.

In 1940 the Williamson pipe was discovered in *Tanzania*. It is the largest in area in the world and greatly increased the country's production; 65 per cent of the output is of gem quality.

The Orapa Mine in *Botswana* has been in production since 1967; not above 15 per cent is of gem quality but other pipes seem more promising.

Diamond mining is very extensive in *Siberia* particularly from the pipes in the Yakutia area, of which the Mir pipe is the best known. The U.S.S.R. is the second largest producer of gem and industrial diamonds after South Africa.

The exhibit includes a series of models of some of the largest and most famous diamonds which have been found from time to time at the various localities.

Of special interest is the 'Koh-i-Noor', which came into the possession of the East India Company in 1849. It was presented to Queen Victoria in 1850 and was recut in 1852 when its weight was reduced from 191 metric carats to 108.8 metric carats.

The largest diamond found hitherto is the famous 'Cullinan', models of which—presented by Messrs. Levy and Nephews—are exhibited here. It was found on the 26th January, 1905, in the yellow ground of the Premier Mine, near Pretoria, and was named after Sir T. Cullinan, the Chairman of the Company. The rough specimen was apparently only a part of a crystal and weighed 3,106 metric carats, which is equivalent to 621.2 grammes, or nearly 1 lb 6 oz avoirdupois. It was presented in 1907 to King Edward VII, and was cut by the firm of Asscher and Company, Amsterdam.

Two large and magnificent brilliants, one a drop-shaped brilliant or pendeloque, seven smaller stones and ninety-six still smaller brilliants were the result of this operation, the total weight of cut material being 1,063.4 metric carats, which is equivalent to a yield of $34\frac{1}{4}$ per cent of the rough material. The large pendeloque, weighing 530.2 carats, or just under a quarter of a pound, is the largest cut diamond in the world.

A tray of stones all cut to the same diameter shows a collection of materials intended to simulate diamond.

Corundum (CASES 3A and 4A)

Hardness, 9; Specific gravity, 4.0; Doubly refracting; Refractive Index, 1.77–1.76; Birefringence, 0.008.

This mineral species occurs in several varieties, all of which consist essentially of aluminium oxide or alumina, crystallise in forms belonging to the trigonal system, and possess similar hardness and specific gravity. Common corundum, more particularly the compact, impure, granular variety known as *emery*, is extensively used as an abrasive on account of its hardness.

Transparent corundum exhibits an exceedingly wide range of colours and comprises some of the most costly and popular gemstones on the market, the most important of these being *ruby* or transparent red corundum, and *sapphire*, the transparent blue variety. 'Sapphire' is also used with an appropriate adjective for the other colours: purple, sapphire, yellow sapphire, white sapphire, etc. Terms such as 'oriental topaz' and 'oriental amethyst', meaning yellow and purple sapphire respectively are also frequently met with but their use should be discouraged. The causes of these remarkable variations in colour are obscure and appear to be due to small traces of different metallic oxides such as the oxide of chromium in the case of ruby and the oxides of iron and titanium in the case of blue sapphire. Zones of different colours are sometimes present in one stone, whilst sometimes a cut specimen owes its tint to a small spot of colour situated near the base of the stone so that much of the light reflected from the bottom facets passes through it, acquires its colour, and reaches the observer through the top facets.

Ruby varies in colour from pale-pink to deep-red, the tint known as *pigeon's blood*, a deep-red tinged with purple, being most admired and often occurs in Burmese stones. Flawless specimens showing the correct colour are rare and, with the exception of emerald, are perhaps the most valuable gemstones used in jewellery. They may be cut as brilliants but more often the mixed cut, with the crown as in a brilliant and the base cut in steps is preferred. Ruby shows pronounced dichroism, the images seen in the dichroscope being deep red tinged with purple and yellowish red respectively. The deep red colour corresponds to the light travelling along the optic axis of the crystal, i.e. in a direction perpendicular to the basal plane, and on this account a cut stone shows the best colour when the table is parallel to that crystal face.

Whilst not so valuable as the ruby, *sapphire* is a popular stone which commands a high price for good specimens. It varies in colour from a pale, cornflower-blue to a deep velvety-blue and, like the ruby, shows pronounced dichroism. In the dichroscope it gives a deep blue and a greenish or yellowish blue image. The deeper colour corresponds to the light travelling along the optic axis and a stone is usually cut so that the table is perpendicular to that direction, i.e. parallel to the basal plane.

Sapphire and ruby occasionally show a silky structure and sometimes they are penetrated by a series of minute canals running approximately parallel to the prism faces of the crystals and so intersecting at angles of 60°. These specimens, when cut *en cabochon*, show a six-rayed star or an opalescent appearance in reflected light and are known as *star rubies* and *star sapphires*. Examples are shown here.

The characteristic features of cut specimens of corundum are their strong vitreous lustre and refraction, weak dispersion, extreme hardness, high specific gravity, their double refraction and, when coloured, their dichroism. These properties serve to distinguish ruby, sapphire, yellow and green sapphire from stones like spinel, garnet, tourmaline, topaz and emerald for which they might be mistaken. The absorption spectrum of ruby is very characteristic. In addition to a broad band covering the yellow and green parts of the spectrum and narrow bands in the blue and orange-red there is a narrow band, actually a doublet, in the deep red, which by scattered light appears as a *bright* band. This fluorescent effect is due to the re-emission of the absorbed light.

The methods of distinguishing natural from artificial corundum have already been described (p. 25).

Mogok in Upper Burma is the most renowned locality for ruby where the stones occur in a crystalline limestone of Upper Cretaceous age. This rock weathers to a yellow clay containing ruby, sapphire, red spinel, tourmaline, and other minerals. Thailand and Cambodia are famous for sapphires which occur, associated with ruby and other varieties of corundum in small basaltic bodies near the Thai-Cambodian border; the district around Chantabun, near Bangkok, yields rubies but of poorer quality than the Burmese stones. The celebrated gem-bearing gravels of Rakwana and Ratnapura in Sri Lanka yield large numbers of coloured gemstones, including sapphire of various colours; ruby is, however, rather rare. Other localities for sapphire illustrated here are East

Africa, Montana, U.S.A., Kashmir, and Anakie in Queensland.

Beryl (CASE 5A)

Hardness, 7¾; Specific gravity, 2.90–2.68; Doubly refracting; Refractive Index, 1.59–1.57; Birefringence, 0.005–0.009.

This mineral species includes not only the dull, turbid, common beryl, of frequent occurrence in granitic rocks, but also a number of transparent, precious varieties prized for their beautiful colours and used extensively as gemstones. All the varieties consist of a silicate of beryllium and aluminium carrying traces of impurity which probably cause the tints and crystallise in hexagonal, columnar crystals which possess indistinct cleavage parallel to the basal plane.

The best known of the precious varieties of beryl are *emerald*, characterised by its beautiful green colour, and *aquamarine*, in which the tint varies from pale-blue to greenish blue; *golden beryl*, or *heliodor*, as its name implies, is yellow in colour, whilst the name *morganite* is sometimes applied to the pink variety.

For perfect specimens *emerald* is, perhaps, the most expensive stone at present on the market. It shows variations in colour from darker to paler shades, the tint most admired being a dark 'velvety-green', which also suggests the lustre of a good specimen. The colour tolerates strong heat and is probably due to the presence of small amounts of chromium. With the dichroscope, the images are coloured yellowish green and dark bluish green. Flawless stones are extremely rare and most specimens are marred by cracks and inclusions which greatly lessen their transparency and value. Emerald is usually step-cut but it may also be cut *en cabochon*, or as a brilliant.

The distinguishing features of emerald are its low specific gravity, its comparative softness, and its dichroism. These properties are quite sufficient to discriminate between it and any other superficially similar stone. The green corundum, or 'oriental emerald' (p. 36) is harder and heavier; the green garnet, or *demantoid* (p. 51) bears a strong resemblance to emerald, but it lacks dichroism and is heavier; green tourmaline, diopside, peridot, and hiddenite, amongst other stones, may be confused with emerald, but they have a higher specific gravity. A green paste is made which is difficult to tell from the genuine stone by inspection, but it has no dichroism and is softer. The Chelsea colour filter may distinguish between emerald and most of the other stones. Through the filter emerald appears red, whereas the other stones remain green: demantoid may also appear of pink or reddish colour. Synthetic emerald, only produced on a commercial scale in recent decades, may be distinguished from natural stones by the presence of typical minute liquid inclusions in veils, visible with a strong lens or low-power microscope. The specific gravity, 2.64–2.66, is very similar to that of quartz and distinctly lower than that of natural emerald, and the refractive indices are also lower than those of natural stones.

Unlike most gemstones, emerald is not found in sands and gravels and is always mined from the parent rock. A principal modern source is Muzo, Colombia, where the crystals occur in calcite veins in a bituminous limestone, with pyrites, quartz and parisite, the rare carbonate of cerium, as associates. Other localities are Egypt, probably the original source of emerald, Habachthal in the Tyrol, the Ural Mountains, Brazil, Zimbabwe (formerly Rhodesia) and Zambia; mica-schist is the parent rock in all these cases, and the stones are often inferior to the Colombian ones. At Emmaville, New South Wales, emeralds of poor quality occur in granite.

Aquamarine possesses the same chemical composition and crystal form as emerald, but is characterised by its pale bluish green or blue colour. The tints have been ascribed to the presence of small amounts of iron. In contrast to the emerald, it is frequently found in large, transparent masses, free from flaws, and consequently its value is very much lower. Faults are, however, common enough and usually take the form of cavities and striae, as seen in one large cut specimen in the centre of the tray. Dichroism is observable in all except the very pale stones, the dichroscope yielding a pale blue and a yellowish green or practically colourless, image. Aquamarines are brilliant or step-cut and examples of these are shown here. The low specific gravity is usually sufficient to distinguish these pale varieties of beryl from any stone, e.g. blue topaz or euclase, which outwardly resembles them.

The home of the aquamarine is in the cavities of granitic rocks. Many of the specimens in the case came from Adun Tschilon in southern Siberia, where the beryl occurs in the cavities of a quartz-topaz rock penetrating granite. Examples are also shown from Sverdlovsk in the Urals and from the Mourne Mountains, Ireland.

Specimens of yellow beryl (heliodor) and pink beryl (morganite)—a variety found in Madagascar—are also exhibited.

Tourmaline (CASE 5B)

Hardness, $7\frac{1}{4}$; Specific gravity, 3.15–3.0; Doubly refracting; Refractive Index, 1.64–1.62; Birefringence, 0.018.

This stone has a most complicated chemical composition, which varies widely in different specimens. Corresponding to the variations in composition there are distinct differences in specific gravity and in colour, so that this stone differs from many others in that its tint is not due to traces of impurity, but is, to some extent, an expression of its chemical composition. Tourmaline is a complex silicate of boron and aluminium with magnesium, iron and the alkali metals, i.e. sodium, potassium and lithium, present in variable quantities; calcium may also be present. Iron-tourmaline is usually black, alkali-tourmaline may be red, green, or colourless, and magnesium-tourmaline, yellow, brown, or even black. There is, however, no hard and fast line between these rough divisions which grade into one another.

Despite their wide differences in composition, all varieties unite in having the same crystalline form. The crystals belong to the trigonal system, and usually take the form of prisms terminated by one or more sets of rhombohedral faces. The prisms are roughly three-sided in section, and bear deep vertical striations which are well seen in the specimens shown in the case.

When terminal faces are present at both ends of the crystal they do not correspond with each other, different faces being developed at each end. This is a manifestation of *polarity* which is also revealed in the other physical properties. One effect of this polarity is that tourmaline readily acquires an electric charge. This may be accomplished by simply rubbing a stone with flannel, or by heating it gently, and letting it cool, when, having become charged, it readily attracts small pieces of paper. This phenomenon is known as *pyro-electricity*.

The commonest variety of tourmaline is the black *schorl* which is quite opaque, and never used as a gemstone. It is represented here by a good suite of specimens, including some from Bovey Tracey, Devonshire.

The clear, transparent, precious tourmaline shows great diversity of colour and is somewhat extensively cut for jewellery. The following colour-varieties are recognised:—*achroite* or colourless tourmaline; *rubellite* or red tourmaline; *indicolite* or blue tourmaline; green tourmaline has been falsely styled 'Brazilian emerald', 'Brazilian chrysolite', or 'Ceylon chrysolite', depending on the particular shade and on the place where it is found. Crystals sometimes occur in which an outer shell of rubellite encloses a kernel of brown tourmaline or vice versa; specimens are also shown in which the crystals are pink at one end and green at the other. In such cases there are differences in composition between the differently coloured portions of the crystal. Attention may be drawn to the fine suite of specimens from Mesa Grande, Diego County, California, exhibiting this phenomenon, presented by Adolph Tanburn.

Tourmaline is remarkable for its dichroism which, in the deeply coloured kinds, is stronger than in any other gemstone. When, for example, a piece of green tourmaline is viewed in a direction parallel to the prism edge, i.e. along the optic axis, it appears almost black, whilst if it is viewed across the prism edge it has a fine green colour. In every case, no matter what the colour is, tourmaline shows the deepest shade when viewed along the optic axis, and this fact must be remembered when rough material is being cut. Strongly coloured stones must be cut with the table parallel to the prism edge, whilst, in pale stones, the table must be perpendicular to that direction.

Specimens are usually cut in steps with the above mentioned precautions as to the direction of the table, and, with a deeply coloured stone cut in the manner described, the dichroism is quite apparent to the unaided eye. The other optical properties of this mineral call for no special mention: its refractive index is low, its dispersion is weak, and its lustre is of the usual vitreous type.

Tourmaline, presenting as it does so many different colours, has been confused with other stones, from which, however, it can be distinguished by its lower specific gravity, its pronounced dichroism and its refractive indices. These tests are sufficient to discriminate rubellite from ruby, red spinel, and pink topaz, and indicolite from sapphire, and blue spinel The birefringence of tourmaline is considerably greater than that of topaz which has a similar refractive index. Green tourmaline has been confused with peridot, but the latter stone is heavier and shows very weak dichroism. Sometimes, too, it is mistaken for emerald, which is, however, much lighter; the determination of the refractive indices is also a decisive test in distinguishing these minerals.

The mineral is widely distributed, and is found most frequently in granites and gneisses. Brazil, California, Maine, Siberia, Elba, Madagascar all yield tourmaline, examples of which are in the case, whilst it also occurs in the gem gravels of Sri Lanka.

Spinel (CASE 4B)

Hardness, 8; Specific gravity, 3.65–3.58; Singly refracting; Refractive Index, 1.72.

Spinel is the name for a group of minerals which show similar chemical constitution and crystallise in the cubic system. The properties given above apply to precious spinel, the only variety used as a gemstone. It consists of a double oxide of magnesium and aluminium, and frequently carries traces of chromium and iron to which the colours of this mineral have been attributed.

The colour, as seen from the specimens here, shows a wide range with various shades of red common; blue is also fairly frequent, but colourless spinel is rare, at least in specimens large enough for cutting. *Rubicelle* is orange spinel having a pronounced yellow or yellowish red tinge. The term *gahnospinel* has been suggested for those rare blue spinels rich in zinc. They cannot be distinguished from other blue spinels with the naked eye, but have, according to B. W. Anderson and C. J. Payne, who described them, a specific gravity of 3.98 and refractive index of 1.747, both considerably higher than the normal figures. *Ceylonite* or *pleonaste* are names applied to dark green to black stones.

The brilliant and step-cut are used with spinel, but the mixed cut is exceedingly common, and most of the examples in the case have been treated in that way.

Spinel is distinguished from nearly every stone which it resembles by its single refraction and consequent lack of dichroism. The dichroscope alone is sufficient to determine spinel from ruby, sapphire and tourmaline. To discriminate between spinel and garnet is not so easy, as they are both singly refracting, but determination of the specific gravity and refractive index should remove any doubt. Synthetic spinels, made by the Verneuil process described in Chapter 4, are similar to the natural stones but may be distinguished under the microscope by the absence of natural features such as straight colour-banding and crystal inclusions, and by the presence of occasional bubbles. They are usually made, however, to simulate ruby and sapphire, not natural spinel, and may be easily distinguished from these by refractive index, specific gravity and, usually, a distinct difference in colour.

Synthetic blue spinel, coloured by cobalt, may be distinguished from natural blue spinel and other blue stones by its absorption spectrum which shows three bands in the orange, yellow and green. The Chelsea colour filter is also useful: the cobalt which gives synthetic spinel its colour makes it appear red through the filter, whilst most other similarly coloured stones remain blue.

The physical constants of synthetic spinel are appreciably higher than those of the natural stones, the refractive index usually being near 1.73 and the specific gravity about 3.63.

Euclase (CASE 4B)

Hardness, 7½; Specific gravity, 3.1–3.05; Doubly refracting; Refractive Index, 1.67–1.65; Birefringence, 0.019.

This mineral occurs sparingly and is very rarely cut for jewellery. It consists of a silicate of beryllium and aluminium with water and is found in crystals belonging to the monoclinic system. Euclase may be quite colourless, but it usually shows a very delicate green, bluish green or blue tint stongly reminiscent of the aquamarine. Such coloured material is distinctly dichroic. Examples are shown from Governador Valadares, Brazil.

Taaffeite (CASE 4B)

Hardness, 8; Specific gravity, 3.60; Doubly refracting; Refractive Index, 1.72; Birefringence, 0.004.

Only a few examples of this stone are known. The first was picked out, in 1945, from amongst some spinels by Count Taaffe, a keen Dublin gemmologist, who noticed the small double refraction. It is a beryllium magnesium aluminate and crystallises in the hexagonal system.

Phenakite (Case 4b)

Hardness, $7\frac{3}{4}$; Specific gravity, 2.96; Doubly refracting; Refractive Index, 1.68–1.66; Birefringence, 0.016.

Phenakite consists of a silicate of beryllium and crystallises in the trigonal system. It is usually colourless, but yellow or pink phenakite is sometimes found. The natural crystals shown here have rather a dull appearance, but the fine brilliant-cut specimen, weighing 20 carats, shows the high lustre which is brought out by polishing. Phenakite occurs at various localities, but it has little importance as a gem. Specimens are shown from Takovaya, Sverdlovsk in the Urals, where crystals of considerable size are found in a mica-schist.

Sphalerite (Case 4b)

Hardness, $4–3\frac{1}{2}$; Specific gravity, 4.10–4.08; Singly refracting; Refractive Index, 2.37.

Sphalerite, or zinc blende, crystallises in the cubic system. A common ore of zinc but the gem quality material, often a rich yellow, comes from Picos de Europa, Spain; the lustre and high dispersion, 0.156, are noteworthy.

Chrysoberyl (Case 4b)

Hardness, $8\frac{1}{2}$; Specific gravity, 3.74–3.64; Doubly refracting; Refractive Index, 1 76–1.75; Birefringence, 0.009.

Chemically this mineral is closely related to the spinels, as it consists of a double oxide of beryllium and aluminium. It differs from members of that series, however, in crystallising in forms belonging to the orthorhombic system. The crystals may be simple but twinning is common and gives rise to complicated forms having a hexagonal appearance as shown by some of the specimens in the case.

Typical chrysoberyl has a yellow colour which may vary from a fine golden tint to yellowish green or pale green: the yellowish green colour is the commonest. The colour in this chrysoberyl is never very intense, and the stones show weak dichroism.

In the *cymophane* or as it is alternatively called, *cat's-eye chrysoberyl*, a large number of minute canals, arranged in a regular manner cause a band of light or, at least, an opalescent sheen, when the stone is cut *en cabochon*. Cymophane cut in this style resembles cat's-eye quartz (p.64) but possesses a superior chatoyancy and may be distinguished from quartz by its greater hardness and specific gravity.

Alexandrite is dark green chrysoberyl characterised by strong dichroism; in the dichroscope one of the images is green whilst the other is pinkish red. This variety has the curious property of appearing green by daylight and red by tungsten light, a property explained by the strong absorption of light in two bands of the spectrum. These absorption bands exist in the blue and in the yellow parts of the spectrum so that the light which emerges from the stone consists to a large extent of green and red rays. If the stone is examined in light rich in green rays, it appears green, whilst, if the light is rich in red rays, the stone appears red.

Chrysoberyl, when transparent, is cut in any of the styles referred to in connection with other coloured stones ; step-cut, mixed cut and brilliant cut specimens are exhibited.

The yellowish green varieties have often been mistaken for *peridot*, but, as the latter stone has a hardness of only $6\frac{1}{2}$, a specific gravity of 3.3 and refractive indices 1.66–1.69, the two are easily distinguished.

Yellowish green *spodumene* (p.53) also has been confused with chrysoberyl, but it is lighter (specific gravity, 3.18), softer (hardness, $6\frac{1}{2}$–7), and has lower refractive indices (1.66–1.68).

Transparent chrysoberyl comes from the Minas Novas district of Brazil, where it is associated with spodumene. Good specimens of transparent chrysoberyl as well as cymophane are found in the gem-gravels of Sri Lanka.

The original locality for alexandrite was the right bank of the Takovaya River, east of Sverdlovsk in the Urals, where the mineral occurs associated with emerald in a mica-schist. Specimens from this locality are shown, and it will be seen that they have the complex hexagonal form mentioned above. They are usually much fissured and a very small proportion of the material is suitable for cutting. The locality was discovered in 1830 on the day when the Tsar Alexander II came of age, and the variety was named after him.

Alexandrite of gem-quality is also found in Sri Lanka and Zimbabwe, and some of it shows a chatoyancy similar to that of the cymophane. A chatoyant alexandrite is exhibited. A fine set of chrysoberyl jewellery is shown, given by his widow in memory of Dr E. H. C. Rutland.

Cassiterite (CASE 4B)

Hardness, $6\frac{1}{2}$; Specific gravity, 7.0–6.8; Doubly refracting; Refractive Index, 2.09–1.99; Birefringence, 0.096.

Very occasionally, cassiterite, or *tinstone*, the principal source of the valuable metal *tin*, occurs in pieces of sufficient size and purity to be cut. The resulting gemstone, which is of yellowish or brownish colour, is frequently very attractive. The mineral is of very simple chemical composition, being an oxide of tin, and crystallises in the tetragonal system. The properties of cassiterite are so distinctive that little difficulty should arise in identifying it. The very high specific gravity, greater than that of any other gemstone, serves to separate cassiterite from sphene, with which it might be confused.

Cassiterite occurs in many parts of the world in rocks genetically related to granite and in alluvial and eluvial deposits derived from them.

Topaz (CASE 3B)

Hardness, 8; Specific gravity, 3.56–3.50; Doubly refracting; Refractive Index, 1.63–1.62; Birefringence, 0.008.

A fine series of specimens of this mineral, both cut and in the rough, is shown here. Topaz is one of the very few precious stones of any importance containing fluorine as a principal constituent, this element is combined with alumina and silica to form a fluo-silicate of aluminium; a small amount of water is also present.

Topaz is frequently found in fine, bold crystals which belong to the orthorhombic system. The prism faces are always well developed and are usually striated in a vertical direction. The crystals are almost always attached to the parent rock by one end of the prism and doubly terminated ones are rather rare. They can be split with the greatest of ease into plates parallel to the basal

1 Corundum Ruby crystal in matrix (top left), rough sapphire (top centre), three corundum crystals (right), and cut stones

2 Beryl group, including emerald crystal in calcite (top centre), aquamarine crystal (right), and cut stones

3 Olivine (peridot), spinel, chrysoberyl and sinhalite Olivine, crystal and cut stone (top left); sinhalite (bottom left); spinel, octahedral crystal and six cut stones (centre); and chrysoberyl, alexandrite crystal in schist (top right), and five cut stones (right)

4 Topaz and tourmaline The seven crystals and stones on the left are topaz; the remainder are tourmaline including schorl (top right), and rubellite (centre)

plane, and this property renders cut specimens somewhat fragile and liable to fracture when subjected to a sudden shock.

The range of colour in topaz is not so wide as in some gemstones, but an interesting suite is presented by the specimens shown here. The majority of the rolled pebbles are colourless, and stones cut from such material may be mistaken for diamond, rock crystal, or white corundum.

Diamond has a similar specific gravity but is much harder and shows greater fire; rock crystal is softer and lighter; and white corundum is harder and heavier. Determination of the refractive indices also serves to distinguish topaz from these stones.

Yellow is the typical colour of topaz, so much so that, as already mentioned (p. 35), the name has been applied to yellow corundum, and to yellow quartz, with somewhat confusing results. The tint varies in intensity from the merest tinge to the deep, yellowish brown seen in one or two of the cut specimens on the tray, whilst a distinct reddish brown is observable in some of the crystals from Brazil.

The fine, greenish blue colour of the Siberian crystals is almost identical with that of the aquamarine, and it is impossible to distinguish cut specimens of the two stones by mere inspection; aquamarine is much lighter than topaz, is a little softer and has lower refractive indices. Topaz may be confused with tourmaline, which has similar refractive indices, but topaz is heavier and, having a lower birefringence than tourmaline, shows less clearly separated shadow edges on the refractometer.

Natural crystals of a pink colour are rare, but a good example from Brazil is shown here. The fine pink stones sold as *rose topaz* are all produced by the heating of yellow ones (p. 25).

Dichroism is shown by most coloured topazes, but, even in the more deeply-tinted specimens, it is never apparent to the unaided eye, although it is distinct in the dichroscope. With yellow stones, the images are dark and pale, and sometimes one of them is distinctly pink; the pale blue stones give a faint-pink and a blue image; whilst with rose topaz, the images are fairly deep pink and practically colourless.

The refractive index is low, the dispersion is weak, and the lustre is of the usual vitreous type. Colourless topaz, therefore, presents no particularly striking features, and it is the coloured varieties which are chiefly used in jewellery. These are cut in steps with a small table, but examples cut as brilliants are also shown.

Topaz is usually found in granitic and gneissic rocks and sometimes it occurs as rolled pebbles in the beds of rivers. Many of the fine brown crystals come from the neighbourhood of Ouro Preto, in the south-west of Minas Gerais, Brazil, where they occur, associated with quartz, in a decomposed clay-slate. At Mursinska in the Ural Mountains, topaz of a fine blue colour is found associated with beryl, quartz and feldspar in the druses of the granite. Beautiful transparent crystals are shown from this locality and also a large colourless one from Miask, another locality in the Urals. There is also a fine group from Adun Tschilon in Transbaikalia, where quartz and topaz form a topaz-rock. (See *Beryl*). A fine step-cut blue stone from Teofilo Otoni, Brazil, is exhibited.

A fine water-worn boulder from Brazil weighting 29½ lb (13.4 kg) is displayed on a pedestal adjacent to the case. It consists of a single crystal and shows the perfect cleavage of the mineral.

Olivine, Peridot (CASE 2B)

Hardness, 6½; Specific gravity, 3.46–3.35; Doubly refracting; Refractive Index, 1.69–1.65; Birefringence, 0.038.

Olivine consists of a silicate of magnesium and iron, and, as the ratio of the amounts of these two metals varies considerably, differences in specific gravity and intensity of colour are found.

This mineral normally shows a yellowish green to leek-green colour with none of the wide variations so prominent in many gemstones. The name, *peridot*, is applied to the dark-green variety illustrated here by cut specimens, whilst the name *chrysolite* has been given to stones of yellowish green colour. Unfortunately, chrysolite, which in America particularly has been used as a synonym for olivine, has been applied to many stones since first used by the Greeks, and its use is best discontinued.

The crystals belong to the orthorhombic system and are sometimes, like those in the collection, flat and platy with the large prominent face vertically striated.

Olivine is dichroic, a property which is more pronounced in the dark leek-green *peridot* than in the paler, yellowish green varieties. The images in the dichroscope are coloured yellow and green respectively. The lustre is vitreous, but cut specimens, especially if the colour is deep, have a somewhat oily appearance which is characteristic, and can be seen here. The refractive index is not high, and the dispersion is weak, but the beautiful body-colour makes the appearance of a cut peridot very appealing. Reference has already been made to several of the stones which may be confused with peridot. They include green corundum, chrysoberyl and emerald, from all of which it can be distinguished by its specific gravity and refractive indices. The same properties discriminate it from green garnet and tourmaline, both of which are described elsewhere (pp. 38, 51).

Olivine is widely distributed in various igneous rocks, but always in grains or small crystals which are useless for the purposes of jewellery. Specimens of sufficient size and transparency for cutting have been found in the parent rock at only one locality, namely, the Island of St John, in the Red Sea, where crystals occur in the cavities of an olivine-rock, or *dunite*, which is much decomposed and serpentinised. The large beautifully coloured stone from this locality shown in the case weighs 146 carats.

Sinhalite (CASE 2B)

Hardness, 6½; Specific gravity, 3.49–3.47; Doubly refracting; Refractive Index, 1.71–1.67; Birefringence, 0.038.

Long thought to be brown peridot, sinhalite was first proved to be a new mineral in 1952. The specific gravity is higher than that of peridot but the other constants are similar. Chemically it is a magnesium aluminium iron borate and crystallises in the orthorhombic system. The name is taken from an old name for Sri Lanka which is the usual locality. Examples are shown.

Zircon (Case 2b)

Hardness, $7\frac{1}{2}$; Specific gravity, 4.69–4.0; Doubly refracting; Refractive Index, 1.99–1.92; Birefringence, 0.059.

This stone is a silicate of zirconium and occurs widely disseminated in granites and gneisses, usually in the form of dull, opaque crystals which are useless for decorative purposes. The crystals belong to the tetragonal system and commonly take the form of prisms terminated by a four-sided pyramid. The clear, transparent precious zircon almost always occurs as rounded crystals and pebbles in sands and gravels, and samples of such material from various localities are shown here. The colour exhibits a wide range, and one or two names have been applied to different varieties. Thus *hyacinth* or *jacinth* is the fine red to brown zircon, whilst pale-yellow to colourless stones are known as *jargoons*; in addition to these, zircons of various other tints, e.g. fine green, golden-yellow, puce-coloured, are represented. Specially interesting are the blue and greenish blue zircons. Unlike the other colour-varieties of this mineral, which are not sensibly dichroic, they show strong dichroism and yield a deep-blue and pale-blue image in the dichroscope. The deeper tint corresponds to light travelling along the optic axis and, consequently, the best effects are achieved in the cut stone when the table is perpendicular to that direction. These blue zircons are obtained by heating brownish-coloured stones, and colourless stones are also prepared in this way.

The properties of zircon show an extraordinarily wide range, and it is possible to distinguish a 'normal', or 'high', and a 'low' type. In the normal type, the mineral is completely crystalline, or nearly so, whereas in the low type the crystal structure has broken down to an amorphous or semi-amorphous state, due to radio-activity.

The specific gravity of normal zircon is about 4.69, the refractive indices 1.92–1.99 and the birefringence 0.059. In the low type, which is always of some shade of green, the specific gravity is only about 4.0 and the refractive index 1.79. The birefringence is very low and the hardness less than that of the normal zircon.

Intermediate varieties having properties between the normal and low types are also known, and these may be converted to the high variety by heating. Some low zircons may also be converted in this way.

Ordinarily, only heat-treated stones are met with in jewellery and usually are not difficult to identify. The frequently characteristic colour, almost adamantine lustre and strong double refraction all serve to identify the species. The double refraction is so strong that if the back of a stone is viewed through the table face, the edges of the facets are seen as double lines. In addition to these properties, the specific gravity also distinguishes zircon from similar stones. Owing to its high refractive index, which is greater than that of most commercial refractometers, zircon does not give a reading on these instruments.

A useful confirmatory test is examination of the absorption spectrum. Zircons do not always show this spectrum but when they do it is very characteristic. It consists of a considerable number of fairly narrow bands occurring from one end of the spectrum to the other. Even when these are not well developed the strongest, in the orange-red, may often be faintly seen. This band is always shown by heat-treated stones.

The rare low variety of zircon may be difficult to identify, but determination of its properties should remove any doubt as to its nature. In place of the narrow spectral absorption band in the orange-red characteristic of normal zircon, it shows a broader, less well defined band.

The brownish coloured stones which have been heat-treated come from Indo-China. The diggings are in the Mongka district of eastern Cambodia and the stones are treated and cut in Bangkok, Thailand.

Idocrase (CASE 2B)

Hardness, $6\frac{1}{2}$; Specific gravity, 3.4–3.3; Doubly refracting; Refractive Index, 1.72–1.71; Birefringence, 0.004.

Idocrase, also known as vesuvianite, consists essentially of a silicate of calcium and aluminium with water, and small amounts of ferric oxide, manganese oxide, magnesia, potash and soda. The crystals, which belong to the tetragonal system, usually lack transparency and are commonly of a green or brown colour; yellow and blue tints sometimes occur.

Material suitable for cutting comes from one or two places only, and the stone has quite a restricted use in jewellery. Crystals are shown from Ala, Piedmont, where they occur in chloritic schist with serpentine; cut specimens are also exhibited.

Ekanite (CASE 2B)

Hardness, $6\frac{1}{2}$; Specific gravity, 3.28; Singly refracting; Refractive Index, 1.60.

Ekanite is a rare metamict calcium thorium silicate, of brownish green colour which comes from Sri Lanka.

Kyanite (CASE 1B)

Hardness, 7–5; Specific gravity, 3.68–3.65; Doubly refracting; Refractive Index, 1.73–1.72; Birefringence, 0.016.

Kyanite has only a limited use as a gemstone, because of the lack of rough material having the proper colour and sufficient transparency. It consists of a silicate of aluminium, and often carries small amounts of ferric oxide causing the blue colour typical of this mineral. The crystals belong to the triclinic system and are usually elongated prisms flattened prominently parallel to one of the prism faces. If a knife is drawn vertically along the large prism face it scratches it easily, whilst if it is drawn transversely across the face no scratch is made; in the former direction the hardness is 5, in the latter it is 7.

The blue crystals are seldom transparent, and the colour is usually distributed in an uneven manner. Dichroism is quite distinct in the more deeply coloured specimens, the images seen in the dichroscope being light blue and dark blue respectively. Faceted stones are shown.

Andalusite (CASE 1B)

Hardness, $7\frac{1}{2}$; Specific gravity, 3.18–3.12; Doubly refracting; Refractive Index, 1.64–1.63; Birefringence, 0.010.

In composition this mineral is identical with kyanite, but it crystallises in the orthorhombic system. The crystals are prismatic and square in section. the colour may be white, grey, reddish brown, or green, but, as commonly found, andalusite is not transparent enough for cutting. It occurs as rolled pebbles in the sands of Minas Novas, Brazil, the locality which yields most of the material of gem quality. The outstanding feature of andalusite is its strong dichroism. When looked at in one direction, a specimen appears green, whilst in another direction, at right angles to the former, it appears of a rich brownish red colour. In this respect andalusite strongly resembles alexandrite (p. 41), but it can be distinguished by its lower hardness, specific gravity and refractive indices. The cut stones exhibited illustrate the differences in colour found in this mineral.

Sillimanite (fibrolite) (CASE 1B)

Hardness, $7\frac{1}{2}$; Specific gravity, 3.25; Doubly refracting; Refractive Index, 1.68–1.66; Birefringence, 0.020.

Sillimanite, often found as fibres or needles, hence the alternative name fibrolite, occurs in metamorphic rocks (gneisses and schists). It is obtained as orthorhombic crystals or water worn pebbles at Mogok, Burma in association with ruby. The cleavage is very facile and the Burma cut stone shown here, weighing 19.85 carats, is virtually unique.

Kornerupine (CASE 1B)

Hardness, $6\frac{1}{2}$; Specific gravity, 3.32–3.27; Doubly refracting; Refractive Index, 1.68–1.67; Birefringence, 0.013.

Kornerupine, a collector's mineral, is a rare magnesium aluminium borosilicate. It crystallises in the orthorhombic system. The colour is usually brown or green and it comes from the gem gravels of Sri Lanka, the Mogok stone tract of Burma, Madagascar, East Africa and Quebec, Canada.

Epidote (CASE 1B)

Hardness, $6\frac{1}{2}$; Specific gravity, 3.5–3.35; Doubly refracting; Refractive Index, 1.77–1.73; Birefringence, 0.035.

Epidote is seldom used in jewellery. It consists of a silicate of calcium and aluminium in which a proportion of the aluminium is replaced by iron; a certain amount of water is also present.

The crystals belong to the monoclinic system, and, as can be seen from the specimens shown here, are sometimes quite large. They are commonly prismatic with the faces deeply striated parallel to the greater length, and with two directions of cleavage parallel to two faces of the prism. The colour varies with the amount of iron, and the characteristic shade is that known as pistachio-green, but dark green, brownish-green, and black varieties are common, whilst a small cut stone of a clear yellow colour is shown. A feature in epidote is the dichroism which is of the most pronounced type; the two images seen in the dichroscope are coloured respectively green and dark brown. Most of the crystals are too opaque for cutting, but when specimens of sufficient transparency are found they are cut in steps or as flat tables. They may be confused with dark-green tourmaline, but the epidote is heavier and softer.

A noteworthy locality is the Knappenwand, in the Untersulzbachthal, Tyrol, which is the source of many of the large crystals in the collection. Here the epidote occurs as crystals lining the cavities of a rock (an epidotic schist), and associated with calcite, asbestos, adularia, etc.

Zoisite (CASE 1B)

Hardness, 6½; Specific gravity, 3.35; Doubly refracting; Refractive Index, 1.70–1.69; Birefringence, 0.009.

The blue transparent variety of *zoisite*, known as 'tanzanite' from the country of origin, was discovered in 1967. Heat treatment enhances the blue colour and other colours such as green, pink and brown occurring in the same deposits turn blue on heating.

Zoisite is a calcium aluminium silicate, it crystallises in the orthorhombic system; the blue material is strongly pleochroic. It is found over a wide area south of Arusha in Tanzania.

Thulite, the rose-pink variety of *zoisite*, a member of the epidote series, is occasionally cut for ornamental purposes. It comes from Lekevik, east of Trondheim, Norway.

Sphene (CASE 1B)

Hardness, 5½; Specific gravity, 3.53–3.45; Doubly refracting; Refractive Index, 2.06–1.91; Birefringence, 0.120.

When properly cut, sphene is one of the most beautiful of gemstones, as it possesses a high refractive index, very strong dispersion, and pronounced dichroism, a combination of properties which is present in no other member of the series. Unfortunately its hardness is low.

Sphene consists of a silicate and titanate of calcium, and occurs usually in wedge-shaped crystals belonging to the monoclinic system. Much of the material is opaque and unfit for cutting, but beautiful transparent crystals, yellow or green in colour, are found associated with feldspar and chlorite in the Grisons, Switzerland. Other localities are Brazil and Baja California, Mexico.

The cut stones shown here, particularly the large very beautiful brilliant-cut green stone, exhibit in a high degree the dispersion and adamantine lustre of this mineral.

Garnet (CASES 17B and 18B)

This is a name applied to a group of minerals, several of which have been rather extensively used in jewellery. As regards composition, they all consist of a double silicate in which one of the metals may be calcium, iron (ferrous), magnesium, or manganese, whilst the other may be aluminium, iron (ferric), or chromium. So there is calcium-aluminium-garnet, calcium-iron-garnet, magnesium-aluminium-garnet, and so on. These varieties are not sharply separated, but grade into one another, with the result that garnet of one type usually contains varying amounts of the metals which form garnets of another type. Two main groups thus formed have been separated here; the pyrope-almandine-spessartine series in case 17B and the uvarovite-grossular-andradite series in case 18B.

Despite their differences in composition the members of this group all crystallise in the cubic system with the rhombic dodecahedron and the icositetrahedron (Figures 26, 27), either singly or in combination, as the common forms.

Figure 26   Rhombic dodecahedron   **Figure 27**   Icositetrahedron

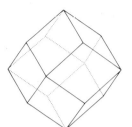

Examples of natural crystals showing these forms are exhibited, and attention may be specially directed to the large, perfect, dodecahedral ones as giving some idea of the size which they attain. Garnet possesses no cleavage, and is singly refracting, but, owing to the differences in composition existing amongst the various members of this group, there is considerable divergence in physical properties. The specific gravity may vary from 3.6 to 4.2, the refractive index from 1.70 to 1.90, and the hardness from $6\frac{1}{2}$ to $7\frac{1}{2}$, whilst the colour, depending as it does on the chemical constituents of the mineral, displays considerable variety of depth and shade.

Garnet is widely distributed in the earth's crust, and is usually found in schists and gneisses, and in limestones which have been acted upon by intrusive igneous rocks; sometimes it is found in serpentine. The greater part of the material is too dull and not sufficiently transparent for cutting, but at several localities beautiful clear stones are found which have been largely used for gems. The gem-varieties of garnet comprise *hessonite, almandine, pyrope, demantoid* and *spessartine*, all of which are differentiated by colour, specific gravity, hardness, and refractive index.

Pyrope

Hardness, $7\frac{1}{4}$; Specific gravity, 3.8–3.7; Singly refracting; Refractive Index, 1.75–1.74.

The magnesium-aluminium-garnet, pyrope, usually possesses the fine, blood-red colour seen in the specimens in the case. Besides these essential metals, pyrope frequently carries variable quantities of calcium, manganese, iron, and chromium, the colour is probably due to the last three of these. This variety is seldom found in distinct crystals and nearly always occurs as grains in association with rocks rich in olivine, or in serpentine which has resulted from the alteration of that mineral.

The chief localities for pyrope are in north-east Bohemia and in East and South Africa. In Bohemia the garnets are picked out of gravels formed by the disintegration of serpentine, and have been extensively used in jewellery. The South African pyrope comes from the diamond mines where it is falsely styled 'Cape ruby'. This is a term introduced in order to sell the stones more easily, and should not be used. Pyrope forms a very effective stone when cut, as it combines a fine colour with absolute freedom from flaws. These stones are usually small and rarely exceed one carat in weight. They can be distinguished from ruby by their single refraction, absence of dichroism, lower specific gravity, and by the fact that the colour is usually tinged with black. With increasing content of iron there is a continuous series from pyrope to almandine and for these intermediate members the term almandine-pyrope is sometimes used.

Almandine

Hardness, 7¼; Specific gravity, 4.3–3.9; Singly refracting; Refractive Index, 1.81–1.75.

Almandine is iron–aluminium–garnet which carries variable amounts of magnesium, calcium and manganese. It has—like pyrope—a deep-red colour, but very often shows distinct tinges of purple which distinguish it at once from that variety. Well marked absorption bands are seen when light transmitted through the stone is examined spectroscopically. There are three main absorption bands, in the yellow, green, and blue-green respectively, as well as a number of other less prominent ones. The high specific gravity is also notable.

Almandine is widely distributed and the crystals frequently are of large size. The parent rock is commonly a mica-schist and attention may be specially directed to the well-formed crystals from Fort Wrangel, Alaska. In Sri Lanka, almandine is found as pebbles in the gravels, and in India it occurs in the disintegration products of mica-schist and gneiss. This variety has often been confused with ruby, but the distinctive absorption spectrum, the low degree of hardness, and absence of dichroism are quite sufficient to distinguish it.

Almandine is treated in many ways as shown by the series of cut specimens exhibited here, and when cut *en cabochon* it goes by the name of *carbuncle*. Several examples of carbuncle will be found in the case. Almandine is often used to cap coloured glass to produce a garnet topped doublet or 'G.T.D'.

Spessartine

Hardness, 7¼; Specific gravity, 4.20–4.12; Singly refracting; Refractive Index, 1.80.

The manganese–aluminium–garnet, spessartine, has usually a red colour and good stones, which have a very beautiful colour, are of considerable rarity. A fine stone weighing 12.01 carats is exhibited in the case.

The principal localities for spessartine are Sri Lanka; Minas Gerais, Brazil; and Virginia and Nevada, United States of America and East Africa.

Grossular

Hardness, 7; Specific gravity, 3.65–3.62; Singly refracting; Refractive Index, 1.74–1.73.

Grossular is a calcium–aluminium garnet; *hessonite* (sometimes called 'essonite') or *cinnamon-stone* is a yellowish red to honey-yellow variety, the colour being due to small quantities of iron and manganese which replace a corresponding amount of calcium. Hessonite possesses the somewhat peculiar property of appearing to greatest advantage under artificial light when it takes on a fine, fiery-red appearance. It has often been confused with the red variety of zircon but its lustre is far inferior, whilst it is much lighter and is singly refracting. Under the microscope, hessonite is seen to contain many small inclusions which give it a granular appearance frequently visible to the naked eye. Nearly all the material of gem-quality comes from Sri Lanka where it occurs as rolled pebbles often of considerable size. Specimens shown include some from this locality as well as green grossular crystals from Siberia. A pale hessonite from Quebec, Canada is very clear.

A massive, often green variety, *hydrogrossular*, occurs in the Transvaal, South Africa; it has been used as a simulant for jade ('Transvaal Jade'). More recently transparent green, yellow and colourless grossular has been found in East Africa; some of it is coloured by vanadium. Green and colourless grossular accompanies the hessonite from Jeffrey Mine, Quebec, Canada; examples can be seen in the case.

Demantoid

Hardness, $6\frac{1}{2}$; Specific gravity, 3.86–3.81; Singly refracting; Refractive Index, 1.90.

This name is applied to the transparent, green variety of calcium–iron-garnet, *andradite*. The colour varies from the deep green of the emerald to the yellowish green of the peridot, and the stone has in consequence been incorrectly called 'Uralian emerald', and 'olivine'. Demantoid has a high lustre, a strong dispersion and refractive index, and these qualities give a very effective appearance to a cut specimen. The hardness is low, and this renders demantoid unsuitable for jewellery which is subjected to hard wear. It may be distinguished from other green gemstones by the high refractive index, high dispersion and absence of dichroism. Specimens from Val Malenco, north Italy are also shown.

Cut and rough specimens are shown from the Bobrovka River, Syssersk, Urals, where the garnet is found as rolled pebbles and also in the parent rock which consists of serpentine associated with dolomite.

Varieties of andradite of other colours are *melanite* (black) and *topazolite* (yellow) examples are included.

The chromium in the *uvarovite* molecule gives to this garnet its typical strong green colour. It is not usually suitable for cutting; localities are the Urals, Siberia; Outokumpu, Finland and Orford, Quebec, Canada.

Cordierite (CASE 18A)

Hardness, $7\frac{1}{4}$; Specific gravity, 2.65–2.58; Doubly refracting; Refractive Index, 1.55–1.54; Birefringence, 0.008.

Iolite and *dichroite* are other names for this mineral which, when cut, is sometimes known as *water-sapphire*. In composition it is a silicate of aluminium and magnesium with water, part of the magnesium being replaced by iron in the ferrous state. It is found in granitic and schistose rocks as large rough crystals belonging to the orthorhombic system, but they, as shown by the specimens here, are usually too dull and opaque for ornamental purposes. At one or two localities, however, material of sufficient transparency for cutting is found, and a few polished specimens are shown, notably the fine stone of 19.7 carats from Burma. The prevailing colour is blue, due probably to the presence of the iron referred to above, but much depends on the direction in which the stone is viewed, as the dichroism of iolite is exceedingly strong, and has given rise to the name *dichroite* already mentioned. In one direction a transparent example appears of a deep blue tint, in another direction, at right angles to the former, it has a pale yellow colour, whilst in yet a third direction, perpendicular to the first two, it appears almost white. As in tourmaline, it is very important to cut the table of a stone in such a way that an observer looking through it may get the fine, intense blue colour, that is, the table must be cut as nearly as possible perpendicular to the first of the three directions enumerated above.

Apart from its remarkable dichroism, iolite shows no property of note. Its hardness, refractive index and specific gravity are low, and its lustre is vitreous, inclined to greasy. The low specific gravity and refractive index distinguish it at once from blue tourmaline and from sapphire. Examples are shown from

Bodenmais in Bavaria, but most of the iolite used for gem-purposes occurs as rolled pebbles in the gravels of Sri Lanka.

Benitoite (CASE 18A)

Hardness, 6½; Specific gravity, 3.68–3.64; Doubly refracting; Refractive Index, 1.80–1.76; Birefringence, 0.047.

This mineral was discovered in 1907 and has since been used as a gemstone, though only to a limited extent. It consists of a silico-titanate of barium, and, in this respect, is related to sphene. It crystallises in the trigonal system and the crystals invariably have a pyramidal aspect with the faces occurring in sets of three. The colour is typically pale to deep blue with a slight violet tint, but colourless crystals are not unknown, whilst, as in the sapphire, blue and white patches may be present in the same crystal. Benitoite is very strongly dichroic; when a crystal is viewed along the principal axis it appears colourless, whilst in a direction at right angles to the axis, it appears of a fairly deep-blue colour. So the table of a cut stone must be ground as nearly as possible perpendicular to the basal plane and not, as in the sapphire, parallel to it. Benitoite has been confused with sapphire, but it is much softer and lighter, and the birefringence is much greater.

The only locality for this mineral is on the west side of the Diablo Range, San Benito County, California, where it occurs in serpentine associated with natrolite, neptunite, amphibole, and various copper minerals.

Axinite (CASE 18A)

Hardness, 7–6½; Specific gravity, 3.29–3.27; Doubly refracting; Refractive Index, 1.69–1.68; Birefringence, 0.011.

Of complex composition, axinite consists largely of a borosilicate of aluminium and calcium with varying amounts of iron and manganese to which the clove-brown colour is probably due. The crystals, which have a very characteristic form, belong to the triclinic system and show exceedingly acute edges. They are usually clove-brown or plum-coloured, and are quite lustrous. The dichroism is strong and the images in the dichroscope may be violet and green or violet and brown according to the observer's viewpoint.

Axinite is sometimes cut *en cabochon*, but the specimens shown here are faceted and they include a rare blue stone from Tanzania. It has a very restricted use as a gemstone.

Many of the finer crystallised examples exhibited here came from St Cristophe Bourg d'Oisans, Dauphiné, France, where they occur in gneiss associated with albite, quartz and prehnite.

The pyroxene group (CASES 17A and 6A)

The minerals of this group are important as constituents of rocks rather than as gemstones, but several of them possess sufficient beauty to warrant their being cut and polished. In composition the pyroxenes are silicates with a general similarity of chemical constitution and they crystallise in forms which, though not identical throughout the series, show pronounced resemblances in interfacial angles and cleavages.

Diopside (CASE 17A)

Hardness, 6–5; Specific gravity, 3.31–3.27; Doubly refracting; Refractive Index, 1.70–1.67; Birefringence, 0.020–0.030.

Diopside is occasionally cut as a gemstone and a few typical specimens are shown here. It belongs to the pyroxene group and consists of a silicate of calcium and magnesium with part of the latter metal replaced by iron in the ferrous state. The colour—which is due to the presence of iron—varies from a very pale green to a deep bottle-green, and crystals are found with the parts near the point of attachment to the matrix deeply coloured, whilst the free end is quite pale to almost colourless; an example of this is shown. The crystals belong to the monoclinic system, are prismatic, and show the two directions of cleavage characteristic of the pyroxene group. They are frequently of fair size, but the larger specimens are usually flawed, and most of the transparent gem-material is supplied by the smaller crystals.

Dichroism is not observable in the lighter varieties, and is very faint in the more deeply coloured ones, so that this property is useful in distinguishing diopside from other stones which are appreciably dichroic; the lustre is vitreous.

Diopside is usually step-cut, and a specimen cut *en cabochon* is shown here. Pale green diopside accompanies the hessonite in the cavities of serpentine at Ala, Piedmont. To distinguish between this stone and peridot is difficult, as they both have weak dichroism and similar specific gravity; peridot is however harder, and shows slightly more dichroism.

Violane, displayed in this case, is a massive violet pyroxene which only rarely has been used for decorative purposes.

Spodumene (CASE 17A)

Hardness, 7–6½; Specific gravity, 3.20–3.15; Doubly refracting; Refractive Index, 1.68–1.66; Birefringence, 0.015

This member of the pyroxene group consists of a silicate of lithium and aluminium, and crystallises in the monoclinic system. The crystals are prismatic and usually flattened parallel to one of the prism faces, whilst they exhibit two directions of perfect cleavage, approximately at right angles and running parallel to the two prism directions. Spodumene is found in pegmatite veins and usually has a dull almost earthy appearance, and a rather pale undecided tint; the rough crystal from Chesterfield, Massachusetts, illustrates this well.

Transparent material is confined to a few localities, mostly in the United States, and is divided into the two colour-varieties, *hiddenite* and *kunzite*.

Hiddenite (or *lithia emerald*) is the transparent green variety containing traces of chromium which forms an effective gemstone when cut and polished. The green crystals are usually quite small and have been found at only one locality, namely Stony Point, Alexander County, North Carolina, where they occur with other minerals in the cavities of a pegmatite. They have a good lustre and show remarkably strong dichroism, the images in the dichroscope being yellow and deep green.

The yellow and green varieties, illustrated here by cut stones and rough specimens, come from Minas Novas, Brazil. They have a strong resemblance to chrysoberyl (p. 41), but are much softer and lighter.

Kunzite is transparent spodumene of lilac-red, violet, or pink colour; it is illustrated here by fine cut specimens, one of which weighs over 424 carats.

Kunzite occurs in California, Afghanistan and Brazil, where it has been found in large crystals, from some of which very fine gems have been cut. Like hiddenite, it exhibits strong dichroism in the more deeply tinted specimens, and it shows strong luminescence when subjected to the influence of radium rays.

Kunzite bears a strong resemblance to pink topaz, but it is softer and lighter.

Enstatite, bronzite, and **hypersthene**, also displayed in Case 17A, are orthorhombic pyroxenes consisting essentially of silicate of magnesium with varying amounts of iron. Enstatite contains the smallest percentage of iron and a green, transparent variety, associated with the diamond in South Africa, has occasionally been cut. It is doubly refracting (refractive index, 1.67–1.66) and dichroic, whilst its hardness is $5\frac{1}{2}$ and its specific gravity, 3.27–3.1; these properties distinguish it from green garnet with which it is sometimes confused. Bronzite (specific gravity, 3.2) and hypersthene (specific gravity, 3.4), which contain increasing amounts of iron, are dark brown in colour and are rarely transparent. They may show a metallic sheen due to the presence of platy inclusions and are occasionally cut *en cabochon*.

Rhodonite Case 18A (specific gravity, 3.68–3.4; hardness, 6–5) is a silicate of manganese crystallising in the triclinic system. Only the fine-grained massive variety is cut, polished and made into ornaments of various kinds, for example, boxes, vases, etc.

The mineral has an attractive, rose-red colour, which is, however, sometimes marred by streaks of black due to alteration. Rough and polished specimens from various localities are exhibited.

Smaragdite, also shown in this case, is a bright green variety of the amphibole hornblende formed by the alteration of pyroxene. It is sometimes worked into ornaments.

Jadeite Jade (CASE 6A)

Hardness, 7–6½; Specific gravity, 3.4–3.3; Doubly refracting; Refractive Index, 1.67–1.65; Birefringence, 0.013.

This mineral has been used from early times for making implements and objects of various kinds, and is used extensively by the Chinese as a medium for all kinds of carvings executed with wonderful skill and much appreciated by European collectors.

Jadeite belongs to the pyroxene group and consists essentially of a silicate of sodium and aluminium, and may be regarded as spodumene in which the former metal replaces the lithium. Frequently, however, there are traces of other metals, such as calcium, magnesium, iron, chromium and manganese, the last three of which cause the colours seen in some of the specimens in the case. Jadeite is rarely found in crystals, but normally as compact, fine-grained and exceedingly tough masses which exhibit a splintery fracture and which sometimes show a tendency to split into plates. The colour is usually white or grey, but various shades of green are frequent, and of these the emerald-green, and a very pale mauve, nearly white, are much esteemed by the Chinese.

A polished plate, having a very pale amethystine colour is shown, whilst two trays of small specimens cut *en cabochon* display some of the varieties of colour.

Two fine polished boulders of jadeite, one adjacent to the jadeite case, also show the variable colour of the mineral. The larger boulder, weighing 176½ lbs. (80.2 kg), has a colour ranging from mottled green to purple, whilst the other in a wallcase, weighing 134 lbs. (60.9 kg), displays deeper shades of green.

The fine emerald-green colour has been attributed to chromium, whilst iron is the cause of the other tints, with the exception of the amethystine one which is possibly due to manganese. Jadeite is translucent to opaque and rarely transparent, whilst the lustre is vitreous inclined to greasy. Thin sections examined under the microscope are seen to consist of an aggregate of fibrous, interlocking crystals of pyroxene; to this matted structure is due the extraordinary toughness of jadeite which is greater than that of steel. It is practically impossible to break up a rounded block with a hammer, and the method usually adopted is to heat it up to a fairly high temperature and then to pour water over it. Jadeite fuses readily before the blowpipe and colours the flame bright yellow, but these and other properties will be referred to when *nephrite*, another mineral with which it is almost invariably confused is discussed.

Implements of prehistoric age made out of this mineral have been found at various, widely separated localities, but the original sources of the material have not yet been discovered. In the Kachin Hills, Upper Burma, jadeite is found *in situ*, and is extensively quarried. Here the mineral occurs, according to the latest view, as an intrusive dyke in serpentine, and associated with albite, chlorite, and amphibolite. Specimens are also shown from Kotaki, Japan, Manzanal, Guatemala and California, U.S.A. *Saussurite*, a rock composed largely of clinozoisite and feldspar can resemble both jades closely: notice the carved leaf dish.

Nephrite Jade (Case 6b)

Hardness, 6½–5½; Specific gravity, 3.0–2.9; Doubly refracting; Refractive Index, 1.63–1.61; Birefringence, 0.025.

This mineral belongs to the amphibole, or hornblende group of minerals and consists of a silicate of calcium and magnesium with a certain amount of iron which is responsible for the colours seen in many of the specimens in the case. Strongly resembling jadeite in general appearance and toughness, nephrite appears to have been applied in the same way by early man for making weapons and objects. The name 'jade' includes both species, but careful chemical and microscopic examination disclosed the fact that under this name two distinct minerals were included; even yet this is not always appreciated and the name 'jadeite' is seldom used by collectors. It may be of interest to summarise briefly the essential differences between the two minerals:

	NEPHRITE	JADEITE
Hardness	5½–6½	6½–7
Specific gravity	2.9–3.0	3.3–3.4
Refractive index	1.62	1.66
	Fusible with difficulty.	Easily fusible.
	Does not colour the flame yellow.	Colours the flame yellow.
Composition	A silicate of calcium and magnesium.	A silicate of sodium and aluminium.

When examined in thin sections under the microscope, nephrite is seen to be built up of interlocking fibres, which, however, do not show the properties of pyroxene, but of amphibole.

From the foregoing account it will be seen that, with rough specimens, the differences between nephrite and jadeite can be established easily. Much of the material, comes to Europe in the form of carvings on which it is difficult to make any test other than that of specific gravity, and even that may be difficult if the specimen is a large one. The absorption spectrum may help. Pale coloured varieties of jadeite show a narrow absorption band in the deep violet. In green stones the general absorption may mask this but then a band may be seen in the deep red.

In external appearance nephrite bears a strong resemblance to jadeite. It shows all colours from pure white to various shades of green, has a somewhat greasy lustre and is translucent to almost opaque. The white variety has little iron and may be regarded as a compact tremolite, whilst the darker ones have a greater content of iron and may be regarded as compact actinolite. Various minerals have been confused with jade, amongst which may be mentioned green serpentine (Case 16B); this is, however, much softer, and can be easily scratched with a knife, whilst jade resists steel. Among other minerals which may be mistaken for jade are green chalcedony (naturally or artificially coloured; Case 14A), aventurine quartz (Case 14B) and grossular garnet (Case 18B).

The best known localities for nephrite are in Eastern Turkestan, and specimens are shown from the old quarries lying in the valley of the Karakash, in the Kuen Lun Mountains. Here the nephrite was found as a layer 20 to 40 feet in thickness associated with gneiss, but the quarries seem to be exhausted. Many other localities exist in the neighbourhood of these mountains, and nephrite pebbles are found in many of the adjoining river beds, and in detrital deposits which are exploited. The material goes to China where it is worked into most intricate and beautiful carvings, examples of which are shown here. Specially noteworthy is the fine flower vase carved in green nephrite.

New Zealand is also a well-known locality which is represented here by a good suite of specimens. The Maoris seem to have appreciated this mineral at an early date and have utilised it for making weapons and ornaments of various kinds. New Zealand nephrite has, typically, a rich green colour, and is found both as rolled pebbles in the rivers and as deposits *in situ* in schist and in serpentine at one or two places in South Island. Examples of the rough material are shown whilst the objects which the Maoris work from it are illustrated by a *tiki*, or idol, one of the finest in existence, a large *adze*, and several ear-pendants. Also of special interest is the fine New Zealand jade box, mounted in gold, graciously lent by H.M. Queen Mary.

Localities long known as suppliers of nephrite are Jordansmuhl, Silesia and Siberia; other sources represented here are Mashaba, Zimbabwe; Eyre Peninsula, South Australia; British Columbia, Canada and Wyoming and California in the U.S.A.

Note the *actinolite* cat's eyes; the fibrous quality which gives rise to the chatoyancy indicates that the material is not sufficiently interlocking in its structure to be termed nephrite.

Meerschaum (Case 16b)

Meerschaum, or sepiolite, is composed of hydrated magnesium silicate. It occurs in porous white, grey or yellowish masses and appears to be formed by the decomposition of serpentine. The hardness of the mineral is 2–2½ and its specific gravity about 2. The principal use is for working into pipes and cigar and cigarette-holders. Eski Shehr, in Asia Minor, is the chief source. *Steatite* or *soapstone*, the massive variety of *talc*, is closely related in composition to meerschaum. It occurs in white, grey, greenish or reddish-coloured masses resulting from the hydration of magnesium-bearing rocks. The specific gravity is about 2.75, whilst the hardness 1, is the lowest on Mohs' scale. Apart from many industrial uses it finds a limited use in ornaments, pipe stems, etc.

Serpentine (Case 16b)

Hardness, 4 (about); Specific gravity, 2.65–2.5.

This material is, properly speaking, a rock, but, as it is used for ornamental objects, e.g. vases and columns, and as it is sometimes substituted for nephrite and jadeite, a short description of its properties may be useful. Serpentine consists of a hydrated silicate of magnesium and usually carries more or less iron. It shows very fine colours which may be green, red, brown, etc., and masses are often mottled in a very beautiful manner (see the specimens in the case and the columns and ornaments in the Main Hall). Green serpentine is very often passed off as 'jade', but the two can easily be distinguished by the test for hardness; serpentine yields readily to the knife whilst jade does not. The mean refractive index ranges in value from 1.49–1.57.

Serpentine has usually resulted from the alteration of rock-masses rich in *olivine*. This mineral consists of a silicate of magnesium and iron, and it is easily decomposed into serpentine and magnetite, i.e. magnetic oxide of iron, a mineral which is usually present as opaque black granules in the altered mass. Such is the origin of the serpentine which occurs in large masses at the Lizard, Cornwall, where it is worked into ornaments, examples of which are shown here.

Bowenite is a pale green translucent variety of serpentine often mistaken for nephrite. It is harder than ordinary serpentine, having a hardness of 5½, but softer than nephrite. Its specific gravity is 2.59 and its refractive index 1.54. Specimens are shown from Rhode Island, United States of America, and from Afghanistan.

Verdite is an ornamental rock of brilliant green colour, containing the green mica *fuchsite*; it is found in the Barberton district of the Transvaal, South Africa.

Prehnite, a hydrated calcium aluminosilicate, pale green or brown in colour, often forms botryoidal aggregates. The green material has been used as jade simulant; rough and worked pieces from Bowling, Scotland, South Africa and Thailand are shown.

Scapolite (Case 16a)

Hardness, 6–5; Specific gravity, 2.70–2.63; Doubly refracting; Refractive Index, 1.57–1.55; Birefringence, 0.023.

Scapolite is the name given to a complex family of minerals composed of alumino-silicates of sodium and calcium and containing chloride, sulphate or carbonate groups. The mineral crystallises in the tetragonal system and, in consequence of its rather variable chemical composition, shows a wide range of optical and other properties. In colour the stones are usually pink, violet or yellow. Note a fine cut stone of weight 77.0 carats and a rough piece of gem quality from Brazil. Specimens from Burma and Madagascar are also shown.

Datolite (CASE 16A)

Hardness, 5; Specific gravity, 3.00–2.90; Doubly refracting; Refractive Index, 1.67–1.63; Birefringence, 0.044.

Datolite, a calcium boro-silicate, chemically similar to danburite, occurs as short prismatic monoclinic crystals. Clear stones are sometimes cut for collectors and one from Bergen Hill, New Jersey, U.S.A. is shown here.

Other tectosilicates have been grouped together in this case. One is *petalite*, a rather glassy looking lithium aluminium silicate; a cut stone from Minas Gerais, Brazil is shown. *Pollucite*, a rare silicate of aluminium and caesium has been cut; an example here is from Newry, Maine, U.S.A.

Dumortierite a fibrous blue orthorhombic mineral is often formed in association with quartz, this makes an attractive rock which is used for carvings; some can be seen here. It is a basic aluminium boro-silicate and comes from Arizona and California in the U.S.A. and also Madagascar and India.

Danburite (CASE 16A)

Hardness, 7; specific gravity, 3.00; Doubly refracting; Refractive Index, 1.64–1.63; Birefringence, 0.005.

In composition, this mineral is a borosilicate of calcium. The crystals belong to the orthorhombic system and resemble those of topaz. They are usually colourless or of some shade of yellow or brown. Although possessing reasonable hardness and fairly high refractive indices, both desirable attributes for a gemstone, danburite is surpassed in colour by topaz and quartz. From topaz it may be distinguished by its lower specific gravity and from quartz by its higher refractive indices and specific gravity.

Three fine cut stones are shown from the principal locality, Mogok, Upper Burma.

Natural glass (CASE 16A)

Natural glass is usually found in the form of the volcanic rock *obsidian* which has a high percentage of silica in its composition and is usually black or grey in colour; the refractive index is around 1.49, the specific gravity varies between 2.42 and 2.33, the hardness is 5. A large proportion of the obsidian used in jewellery comes from North America although it is, of course, found in many volcanic areas.

Pieces of natural green glass found in Czechoslovakia and named *moldavite*, after the River Moldau, have been faceted. They contain characteristic bubbles and swirls. The hardness is $5\frac{1}{2}$, the specific gravity ranges from 2.39 to 2.34 and the refractive index lies between 1.50 and 1.49.

These are thought to be *tektites* which are believed to have an extra-terrestrial origin; other tektites have been found in Thailand, Indonesia and in great quantities over a large part of Australia. The latter, frequently button shaped, are known as *australites*. They appear black or very dark green.

5 Zircon A group showing crystals and cut stones

6 Jade including a nephrite vase, snuff bottle and pendant; and jadeite boulder, necklace, archer's ring and carved praying mantis

7　**Opal group**　Rough and cut stones including fire opal (bottom right)

8　**Quartz group,** including rock crystal, citrine, and amethyst

Another type of natural glass with 98 per cent silica, has been found in the Libyan Desert; it is yellow in colour and has a hardness of 6, specific gravity of 2.21 and the refractive index is 1.46.

The feldspars (CASE 15A and 15B)

This group of minerals is one of the most important and widespread in the rocks of the earth's crust, but few of its members are suitable for use as precious stones. The feldspars are silicates containing at least two metals, one of which is always aluminium, whilst the other may be potassium, sodium or calcium. The group is thus divided into potassium-feldspar, or *orthoclase*, and sodium-feldspar and calcium-feldspar which are known as *plagioclase*. As in the case of the garnet group, however, the feldspars are usually intermixed, with the result that orthoclase often carries appreciable amounts of sodium and calcium, whilst the plagioclase feldspars constitute a series in which sodium-feldspar, or *albite*, stands at one end, calcium-feldspar, or *anorthite* at the other, and between the two are the intermediate members, consisting of mixtures of albite and anorthite in varying proportions.

Orthoclase crystallises in the monoclinic system, plagioclase in the triclinic, but there is a close resemblance between the two sets of crystals. Both possess two principal directions of cleavage which are at right angles in orthoclase, whilst in plagioclase they are slightly oblique. The specific gravity of the feldspars varies from 2.56 to 2.75, the hardness is about 6, and the refractive index is low.

The varieties which have been used for decorative purposes are: Moonstone, amazonstone, sunstone or aventurine feldspar, and labradorite.

Orthoclase (specific gravity 2.56). When orthoclase occurs in clear crystals, it is known as *adularia*; pale yellow crystals (refractive index, 1.53–1.52), from Madagascar, have occasionally been cut; a fine faceted stone of 54.79 carats from here is shown. The name *moonstone* is applied to the variety of feldspar (specific gravity, 2.57) composed of an intimate admixture of orthoclase and albite lamellae which shows a pronounced sheen. The sheen takes the form of a shimmering play of white light which, in some cases, has a distinctly bluish tinge; specimens in which the latter colour is pronounced are the most valuable. Moonstone is almost invariably cut *en cabochon*, when it shows a translucent band grading off into a surround of transparent adularia.

The chief locality is Sri Lanka where the material occurs either as pebbles in the gem-gravels, or as rough fragments in a clay which has probably resulted from the decomposition of an igneous rock.

Moonstone may be distinguished from a glass imitation by its double refraction.

Amazonstone is a variety of the potassium feldspar *microcline* and differs from orthoclase in being triclinic and possessing a fine green to bluish green colour; in other respects, e.g. chemical composition, hardness, specific gravity, it is identical.

Only the deeply coloured specimens have any value as gemstones, and occasionally crystals have been cut *en cabochon*: owing to its opacity, amazonstone is rarely faceted. Large pieces have sometimes been made into vases and other ornamental objects. Crystals occur in the cavities of a coarse granite at Pike's Peak, Colorado.

Sunstone or ***aventurine feldspar*** This variety resembles the similar form of quartz (p. 64) and owes its metallic sheen to the inclusion of small plates of hematite, goethite, or some such mineral, arranged in a parallel manner along the principal cleavage plane of the feldspar.

The aventurine effect is found in several feldspars but is most common in oligoclase (specific gravity, 2.65) which is a sodium-calcium-plagioclase. The specimens shown here are brown, but the colour varies and may be white or greenish.

Sunstone may be distinguished from aventurine quartz by its lower hardness and by the presence of parallel striations on the surface which are the result of the complicated twin structure of the mass.

Among the localities represented here is Arendal, Norway.

Labradorite is arguably the most beautiful of all the varieties of feldspar. It belongs to the plagioclase series and differs from oligoclase in having the percentage of calcium greater than that of sodium; it is consequently a calcium-sodium-feldspar. The specific gravity is 2.70 and the refractive indices 1.56–1.57. Under ordinary conditions it appears to be a dirty-grey colour and has a rather greasy lustre, but, when a suitably cut specimen is observed from different viewpoints, its appearance changes remarkably. The lustre becomes metallic and a beautiful coloured sheen spreads over the surface. The colours vary, but blue, green, and yellow predominate, and various shades of red are sometimes present. The polished specimens in the case have been placed to show the effect well, but the visitor will find that the maximum sheen is obtained in only one position from any specimen; immediately it is looked at from another direction the colours vanish. The sheen is seldom distributed over the surface in a uniform manner, but is interrupted by dull lifeless patches which mar the beauty of the specimen. It is best seen on a cleavage surface and appears to be due in part to the presence of small lamellar inclusions. This explains all the colours except blue which is often found when the inclusions are absent. The blue colours have been attributed to polarisation effects caused by the lamellar structure of the mineral.

Labradorite is usually cut with a flat surface, and has been employed for various ornamental objects; it affords quite an effective medium for cameo-work, as can be seen from the fine examples in the case. The specimens shown here came from Labrador, the original locality, where the mineral occurs in association with hypersthene as rolled blocks lying along the coast.

Cut examples of plagioclase feldspars are shown including clear yellow labradorite from Utah, U.S.A. and the Hogarth Range, Australia, together with oligoclase and albite-oligoclase.

Opal, quartz and other forms of silica (CASES 7, 8, 13 and 14)

Silica, or dioxide of silicon, among the most widespread minerals in nature and, occurring as it does in such a variety of forms, needs a large amount of space to illustrate it. Many of the varieties of silica have been used for ornamental purposes from very early times, but, owing to their abundance, their value is small, and they are employed at present in the cheaper forms of jewellery. Silica may occur in varying degrees of crystallinity. *Opal*, amorphous silica containing a variable percentage of water, is displayed in case 7, very finely crystalline silica designated as *microcrystalline* or *cryptocrystalline* is placed in cases 13–14, and crystalline silica, or *quartz*, in case 8.

Opal (CASE 7A and 7B)

Hardness, 6; Specific gravity, 2.2–1.9; Singly refracting; Refractive Index, 1.45.

Opal is amorphous silica with a variable percentage of water; impurities consisting of the oxides of iron, aluminium, calcium and magnesium are often present. It takes many forms, from the clear, colourless *hyalite* to the white and opaque *milk opal*, and is found chiefly as an alteration product in the cavities of such rocks as andesite and trachyte.

Precious opal, the variety most extensively used as a gemstone, owes its beauty to the remarkable play of colours shown when light falls on the surface of the stone. These colours are due to the structure which consists of closely packed aggregates of minute silica spheres arranged symmetrically and thus producing a diffraction grating effect and hence the rainbow colours. In *harlequin opal* the iridescent areas form a mosaic whilst *flash opal* shows an undivided patch of colour. A square harlequin opal weighing 25 carats is shown.

Black opal, as its name implies, is almost opaque and has a deep-blue to almost black background, with patches showing a magnificent play of colour. The opacity and dark colour are due to impurities. This variety comes principally from Australia. The fine large example shown weighs 131 carats.

When precious opal is heated the play of colour vanishes and the stone becomes lifeless and turbid owing to the expulsion of the water. Some specimens show no play of colours until immersed in water, when they become full of fire which remains for some time after they have been taken out and dried. The effect, however, is temporary and the stone becomes quite lifeless as the water evaporates. These opals are often soaked in oil when they retain their beauty only until the oil decomposes when the whole stone becomes brown and unattractive.

Most of the specimens in the case are cut *en cabochon*, a style which is almost invariably used with this stone in order to show off its beautiful properties. The use of opal as a medium for carving and engraving is illustrated and the inlaid slab shows how specimens with only a thin film of the precious material may be employed. The matrix of one of the cameos has been artificially darkened probably by gentle heating after immersion in oil.

In Queensland and New South Wales precious opal is found in sandstones which may be more or less impregnated with iron as in Queensland or quite white and free from iron as in New South Wales. These sandstones are of Cretaceous age and have had their bedding-planes, joints, and fissures infiltrated with opal at a much later date than their formation. Various examples are shown, one specimen consisting of brown sandstone through which runs a network of fissures now infilled with opal.

Until the discovery of the Australian localities Hungary was the chief source of precious opal and has yielded much material of the finest quality. Here the stone is found filling the fissures and cavities of a decomposed andesitic lava, and is associated with many of the varieties of common opal. The chief locality is near Czerwenitza (now in Czechoslovakia) where the opal is confined to a breccia formed of fragments of the andesite. Iron pyrites is a common associate at this locality.

In Honduras the opal occurs in a decomposed trachyte, but the play of colours in many of the stones from this locality is apt to deteriorate on exposure to the air. Examples are shown from the State of Queretaro, Mexico, where, also, decomposed trachyte is the parent rock.

Fire opal is the transparent or translucent variety which has a reddish brown colour due to the presence of traces of iron. The colour varies from the deeper shades to pale yellow and sometimes is irregularly distributed with dark and light patches appearing on the same specimen. In addition to the main tint, fire opal sometimes shows a play of colours comparable to the precious opal and this property is shown by some of the specimens exhibited here. Well-coloured specimens are cut as brilliants or *en cabochon* when they have a particularly effective appearance.

The chief locality is at Zimapan, in the State of Hidalgo, Mexico, where the material occurs in a decomposed trachytic rock with other varieties of opal as associates.

Opal has been made synthetically; both the black and the white varieties manufactured and presented by Pierre Gilson are shown here.

A glass imitation of opal called 'Slocum Stone' is also shown. Plastic imitations have been made.

Quartz (CASES 8A and 8B)

Hardness, 7; Specific gravity, 2.65; Doubly refracting; Refractive Index, 1.55–1.54; Birefringence, 0.009.

The crystals of quartz belong to the trigonal system, the common form being a hexagonal prism terminated by rhombohedral faces which occur usually in two sets of three, thus giving the appearance of a six-sided pyramid (Figure 28). They possess no cleavage and the prism faces are frequently striated in a transverse direction. Quartz has a vitreous lustre, a low refractive index and weak dispersion. Several varieties of transparent quartz are recognised.

Rock crystal (Case 8B) is clear, colourless quartz, which occurs in crystals varying in size from the merest speck up to those measuring more than a yard in length. A fine group of crystals is exhibited from Dauphiné, France.

Inclusions of other minerals are very common in rock crystal, which often, too, contains cavities filled with gases and liquids. A fine series of specimens illustrating these points is shown here. Especially attractive is the 'Venus' hair stone', in which the enclosed mineral is rutile in golden-yellow needles.

Rock crystal is not much used nowadays as a gemstone, although specimens are occasionally cut as brilliants. Formerly rock crystal was used extensively as a medium for all manner of beautiful carvings, but this art decayed when the manufacture of glass became successful. Now, rock crystal is used for lenses and also has extensive use in the manufacture of crystal oscillators widely used for maintaining a constant frequency in radio transmission. A small plate of quartz in which vibrations have been induced electrically is used to stabilise oscillations to a very constant frequency and so may be used to standardise the frequency of radio waves. Synthetic quartz is widely used: examples are shown.

Rock crystal is very widely distributed, the best examples being found in the cavities of granite and gneiss and in veins and pegmatites. Good specimens are shown from various localities in the Alps, where formerly the material was much sought after. Most of the rock crystal used at present comes from Brazil, which is represented here by a good series of examples, and attention may be called to the large crystal which is mounted on a pedestal adjacent to the case. The quartz crystals come principally from the states of Minas Gerais, Goiaz and

Figure 28   Group of quartz crystals

Baia, and occur in veins, pipes and replacement deposits and in alluvial and eluvial fields. In this country good crystals come from Snowdon, North Wales; the Slate Quarries of Delabole, Tintagel, Cornwall, and many other places. Rock crystal is often known locally as 'diamond' and hence arise such names as 'Cornish diamonds', 'Bristol diamonds', 'Buxton diamonds', etc.

Rock crystal may be distinguished from any other stone by its low specific gravity, its low refractive index, and its lack of fire. A polished sphere of rock crystal in the case reveals the birefringence by the doubling of a cross placed beneath it. The effect is best viewed from directly above, and it will be seen that the separation of the two images is less than in the more strongly birefringent calcite shown in Case 11B.

Smoky quartz (Case 8A) is simply brown coloured rock crystal, and all gradations in colour occur from very faint brown to almost black. The name *morion* is applied to the deeply tinted specimens, whilst *cairngorm* is the reddish brown variety found on the mountain of that name in Banffshire, Scotland.

The very dark specimens when moderately heated, lose a portion of the colouring matter and take on a fine reddish brown to yellow tint. They are then put on the market under such names as 'false topaz', 'Spanish topaz', or 'citrine'.

The natural *citrine* is a yellow quartz which shows the peculiar amethyst structure (see below) and rarely occurs.

Smoky quartz shows dichroism, which is strongest in the deeply coloured specimens. Some of the dark brown stones in the case give, in the dichroscope, a pale yellowish brown and a deep brown image. The paler varieties can be confused with topaz, but the quartz is less hard and not so heavy, and has lower refractive indices.

Smoky quartz resembles rock crystal in its mode of occurrence and specimens are shown from various localities. A large crystal from Switzerland will be found on a pillar adjacent to the case.

Amethyst (Case 8A) is simply purple quartz. The colour varies from very pale violet to deep purple and is often more or less irregularly distributed in the same specimen. Several of the stones here show this, whilst, in others, distinct patches of yellow can be seen. When heated strongly amethyst is decolorised, but, if only a moderate heat is applied, the stone becomes yellow, and is then often sold as citrine. The dichroism of heat–treated amethyst which has turned yellow is not so strong as that of true citrine. In amethyst the dichroism is more or less pronounced according to the depth of colour and some of the darker specimens when examined with the dichroscope show images coloured pale pink and reddish violet respectively.

The crystals of amethyst are similar externally to those of ordinary quartz, but, in many cases, they have a complex internal structure consisting of layers of lamellae in twin position to one another. This is often revealed by striae on the crystal faces and can be seen well in microscopic examination.

Much of the amethyst used in jewellery comes from Brazil where it occurs associated with agate in the amygdaloidal cavities of a decomposed lava. A splendid group of amethyst crystals from Brazil, lent by the Managers of the Royal Institution, is placed in a nearby wall case.

Cat's-eye quartz (Case 14B). In this variety the presence of parallel fibres of asbestos gives rise to a luminous band which is best seen when the specimen is cut *en cabochon*. The asbestos may be weathered out and hollow canals left which give the same effect. The quartz cat's-eye is often confused with the chatoyant variety of chrysoberyl (p. 41), which has a similar appearance and is distinguished as *oriental cat's-eye* or *cymophane*, although the term 'cat's-eye', used alone, should refer to chrysoberyl. The latter stone is much harder and heavier than quartz. Specimens of quartz cat's-eye are exhibited from Sri Lanka, the chief source of this stone, where it is rather highly esteemed. *Tiger-eye* is fibrous quartz of a golden-yellow colour, which gives a beautiful chatoyant effect when cut and polished. This variety owes its origin to the infiltration by silica of crocidolite, a blue, fibrous asbestos which, on oxidation of the iron present in it, has given a brown colour to the mass. When the crocidolite is unaltered, the material has the greenish blue colour seen in some of the polished specimens. It comes from Griqualand West, where it is found as veins in quartz-schist.

Rose quartz (Case 8B), as its name implies, has a delicate pink colour and always appears slightly milky. Exposure to heat or even to strong sunlight discharges the colour. This variety is sometimes cut *en cabochon* and an intaglio in it is shown, also a fine clear stone from Malagasy cut and presented by Dr G. Harrison Jones. Its use as a gemstone is rather restricted.

Aventurine quartz (Case 14B). In this variety enclosed plates of mica give a peculiar gold-spangled appearance to a polished surface in reflected light.

The colour may be reddish brown, yellow or green, and the stone, cut with a flat or slightly rounded surface, is frequently mounted in rings or brooches. The larger pieces are worked into bowls or vases, as demonstrated by the large vase which stands in the centre of the museum. It was presented by the Tsar Nicholas I to Sir Roderick Murchison in recognition of his services to Russian geology. The material consists of micaceous quartz-rock which passes into true aventurine; it was mined at Bieloretsk in the Altai Mountains, and was polished at Tomsk.

Green aventurine comes from India and China, and in China it was much prized and wrought into carvings, examples of which are shown.

A variety of feldspar, known as *sunstone*, or *aventurine feldspar*, strongly resembles aventurine quartz and is used in much the same way, but the quartz is distinguished by its superior hardness.

Examples of *aventurine glass* are shown here. It consists of a readily fusible glass enclosing octahedral flakes of copper and has a much finer appearance than the natural stone. The eye can easily distinguish between the two; the glass is also much softer.

Jasper (Case 14B) consists of massive, compact quartz impregnated with much impurity. This consists mainly of clay and oxide of iron and gives rise to the many colours seen in the specimens exhibited. Red, brown, yellow and green jaspers are common, and were in the past used extensively as ornamental stones.

The chalcedonic varieties of silica (CASES 13, 14)

These varieties have no external crystalline form and appear to be quite amorphous. They have, however, a fibrous structure, clearly visible under the microscope, as the component fibres are doubly refracting and crystalline. The specific gravity, about 2.60, is slightly less than that of quartz whilst the hardness, $6\frac{1}{2}$, is also lower. These fibrous forms are all more or less porous and can be stained by immersion in suitable liquids; many of the bright, vivid colours shown by the specimens here are the result of such artificial treatment.

Chalcedony consists of a mixture of doubly refracting fibres along with more or less opaline or structureless silica. It occurs as botryoidal and stalactitic translucent masses in various kinds of rocks and is usually greyish or bluish in colour. In the form of *agate* (see below) it occurs widely in the amygdaloidal cavities of lavas, and most of the material cut at the present time comes from Brazil, Uruguay, and India. Various colour-varieties are recognised. In *plasma*, the dark green colour is due to inclusions of green earth; such material is occasionally spotted with red and is then known as *heliotrope* or *bloodstone*. *Chrysoprase* is chalcedony stained green with a hydrated compound of nickel; it used to come mainly from Silesia but material of a stronger colour from Queensland, Western Australia and Tanzania is shown. *Sard* (=brown chalcedony) and *carnelian* (=red chalcedony) owe their colour to oxide of iron.

Agate (Case 13A). A fine series, illustrating the mode of occurrence and the applications of this stone, is shown here. It includes an excellent suite of specimens presented by the late Colonel Waldo-Sibthorp.

Agate consists for the most part of chalcedonic silica arranged in bands, often of extreme tenuity, which are distinctly marked off from one another. The differences in the bands arise from varying degrees of transparency and colour. Clear chalcedony may alternate with milky opaline layers and the prevailing tint of the specimen be grey or faint-blue, or strongly marked bands of jasper, carnelian or sard may be present, giving rise to the varieties *chalcedony-agate, jasper-agate,* and *carnelian-agate.*

The home of the agate is in the amygdaloidal cavities of ancient lavas. These cavities were formed by the expansion of the gases occluded in the molten rock and were probably pear-shaped at first, being drawn out by the movement of the viscous mass. On subsequent decomposition of the rock by circulating water, the mineral components were broken down and the siliceous solutions so formed deposited their charge in the steam vesicles in the form of agate. The outer skin of the agate usually consists of a thin coating of *green earth*, or *delessite*, which is derived from the original ferro-magnesian minerals in the lava. This material sometimes projects into the main mass of the agate and gives rise to the peculiar appearance of *moss agate*.

The seat of the agate industry is the town of Idar-Oberstein, situated on the Nahe, a tributary of the Rhine, and about 40 miles from Bingen. The decomposed lava of this district was for a long time the chief source of the rough material and specimens are shown from the hill known as Galgenberg, about two miles from Oberstein. For many years, however, this locality has been exhausted, and the agate is now imported from Brazil, and the neighbouring states of Uruguay and Paraguay. The mode of occurrence in these places is typical and the agates are often found washed out of a red clay derived from the decomposed basalt. A large polished agate from South America is to be seen on a pedestal near the Agate case.

India yields a fair amount of agate from the weathered basalts of the Deccan, and cut and polished specimens from that country are shown here. The chief localities are in the lower valley of the Narbada, where good specimens of *moss agate, mocha stone,* a variety showing arborescent markings of manganese oxide, with *carnelian,* and *heliotrope* are also found.

The amygdaloidal rocks of Scotland yield agate at various places, well-known localities being Montrose, Angus, and in Ayrshire along the coast south of the Heads of Ayr.

Few agates are put on the market nowadays without being artificially coloured. The clear chalcedony layers are more or less porous and absorb the colouring matter whilst the white opaline bands are quite impervious to it. Thus staining not only renders the tint more vivid, but also brings out the zonal structure of the specimen.

The process most widely employed is for the production of the *onyx* of jewellery, i.e. a stone showing alternate bands of black and white and extensively used for such diverse objects as bowls, vases, beads, ashtrays, clocks, handles for sticks, and for cameo-work. The stone is first immersed in a solution of sugar or honey which is kept at a temperature just below the boiling point for several days or even weeks, depending on the porosity of the material. It is then taken out, washed and soaked in warm sulphuric acid. By this means the sugar or honey absorbed from the first bath is converted into carbon which gives the black colour. The fine blue colour seen in the bowl presented by the late Mrs E. Warne is obtained by soaking first in a solution of ferric salt, and then in a solution of potassium ferrocyanide (yellow prussiate of potash), when a deposit of prussian blue is formed in the pores. Green tints are produced by soaking either in a solution of a nickel salt or in a solution of chromic acid and then heated. Similar treatment with a salt of iron causes the chalcedony to assume the colour of carnelian.

The porosity of agate is most important from the commercial point of view and the highest price is always obtained for the rough material which stains most easily. When stained, the stones are cut into the required shapes on large sandstone wheels, polished on wooden cylinders and sent from Idar-Oberstein all over Europe. Most of the 'native pebble' sold at various resorts in Great Britain before the war was simply South American agate cut at Idar-Oberstein.

Lapis-lazuli (CASE 9A)

Hardness, 6; Specific gravity, 2.9–2.7.

Known to our ancestors as sapphire, this stone has been used for ornamental purposes from early times. It is characterised by its beautiful colour which, in the best specimens, is a uniform dark blue of extraordinary depth and intensity. Material of this description is, however, rare, and paler tints—sometimes with a tinge of green—are common, whilst white veins and patches often give the specimen a mottled appearance. The bowl in the case illustrates these points well. One or two of the polished slabs show glistening spangles of iron pyrites scattered over the surface; they give a pleasing appearance although their visual effect can be spoilt by decomposition.

Lapis-lazuli is practically opaque and is consequently never faceted. It has a poor lustre and appears quite dull except on a polished surface. It shows no cleavage and breaks with a splintery fracture displaying a finely granular structure on the broken surface. When examined closely with a lens, or even with the unaided eye, lapis-lazuli appears to be really a mixture of different substances, a fact which is proved by microscopic and by chemical examination. When thin sections are looked at under the microscope they are seen to consist of a matrix of calcite in which are imbedded numerous grains, some of which are colourless, whilst others show various shades of blue.

Chemical examination has proved that the grains really comprise three different minerals: *(a) hauyne*, a silicate of sodium and aluminium with calcium sulphate *(b) lazurite*, a silicate of sodium and aluminium with sodium sulphide, and *(c) sodalite*, a silicate of sodium and aluminium with sodium chloride. In addition to these three minerals there are inclusions of iron pyrites, hornblende and augite. The colour depends entirely on the presence of hauyne, lazurite and sodalite, and as the proportions of these vary in the calcite matrix so do the colour and the percentage composition of the stone. The physical properties of lapis-lazuli also show some variation, and the specific gravity may be as low as 2.45.

Lapis-lazuli is used chiefly for small ornaments such as bowls and vases, though good specimens are sometimes cut with a flat surface and mounted in rings and brooches. Large, well coloured specimens are now somewhat rare and vases are no longer turned out of the massive rock. The lapis-lazuli in most of the modern ornaments is simply a thin veneer cemented on to metal. Lapis-lazuli was formerly used in the production of the artist's *ultramarine*. For this purpose the rock was powdered, washed, and the blue minerals carefully separated. The pigment obtained was very expensive, but now an artificial product, with the same composition as lazurite, is prepared by fusing a mixture of clay, sodium carbonate and sulphur. Examples of the natural and of the artificial ultramarine are placed side by side.

Lapis-lazuli is always found in association with limestone which has been impregnated by the action of some intrusive igneous rock. The chief locality is Badakshan, in Afghanistan, which is the source of most of the specimens shown here. It is also found at the westerly end of Lake Baikal, and in the Andes, Chile. Synthetic lapis-lazuli made by Gilson is shown.

Agate, stained blue artificially, may be confused with lapis-lazuli, but is much harder. The pyrite so commonly present as specks in lapis-lazuli also helps to identify this stone.

Sodalite is occasionally cut for ornamental purposes. Specimens are shown from Ontario, Canada.

Hauyne of sufficient transparency has very rarely been used as a gemstone, and a number of small cut stones are shown.

Tugtupite, found in 1960 in Greenland, is an unusual bright pink colour. It is chemically similar to sodalite and the hardness is $6\frac{1}{2}$ which makes it hard enough for use as an ornamental stone. It usually occurs in massive form.

Fluorspar (CASE 9B)

Hardness, 4; Specific gravity, 3.18–3.02; Singly refracting; Refractive Index, 1.43.

Fluorspar, fluorite or fluor is used to a very limited extent for ornamental purposes. It consists of a fluoride of calcium, and crystallises in the cubic system with fine bold cubes as the typical form. The commonest colour is some shade of purple, but green, brown, yellow, pink, and colourless crystals are found. The pigment may be some colloidal material and heat readily alters the tint of a specimen; examples of specimens which have been subjected to heat-treatment are shown. Though normally too soft for use as a gemstone and difficult to cut on account of its easy cleavage nevertheless some cut stones are shown here.

The dark purple, massive variety, known as 'Blue John' is found only at Treak Cliff, near Castleton, Derbyshire, and has been worked for ornamental purposes for a long time. The larger of the two vases standing on pedestals near the Fluorspar case is considered to be one of the finest examples of this work in existence.

Ordinary crystallised fluorspar is an exceedingly widespread mineral and beautiful specimens have been obtained from the Cornish and Devon mines and from the Weardale district of Durham.

Calcite (CASES 10B and 11B)

The mineral calcite, calcium carbonate, crystallising in the trigonal system, is mainly used for ornamental purposes in the form of marble and onyx marble.

Marble is a crystalline limestone composed essentially of calcite with other minerals present as impurities in varying amounts. The familiar dead white Carrara marble of Italy is an example of the pure carbonate, whilst various coloured impure limestones are shown in the case and forming the decorative screen over the front entrance to the Museum. Note that in commercial usage 'marble' incorrectly implies almost any decorative or building stone which takes a polish. *Onyx marble*, not to be confused with true onyx (p. 66) is a banded, translucent form of stalagmitic calcite. Mexico and Algeria are the sources of much modern material which is used for various ornamental purposes, such as clock-cases, ash-trays, etc.

Marble and onyx-marble may be identified by their hardness, 3, and their effervescence with acid.

Rhodochrosite, a manganese carbonate, has been much used in the stalagmitic banded form. The best material comes from Argentina. A transparent variety is found in the Kalahari region of South Africa.

Malachite, a copper carbonate, is also highly valued as an ornamental stone. An example from Zaire is shown.

Other carbonates, in this case, which have been cut as gemstones, although too soft for normal use are *cerussite*, lead carbonate, *dolomite*, calcium magnesium carbonate, *magnesite* magnesium carbonate and *smithsonite*, zinc carbonate; all have large double refraction. Smithsonite is marketed under the name 'Bonamite'.

Gypsum (CASE 12B)

Gypsum is a hydrated calcium sulphate, and in its massive, compact variety, *alabaster*, is used for interior decorative purposes, for statuary and for carving into ornaments. It may be distinguished from calcite by its lower hardness, 2;

the mineral is soft enough to be scratched with the fingernail.

Two ewers in alabaster will be found on the main staircase above the entrance to the Main Hall. Some sulphates have been faceted and are shown here; *barytes*, barium sulphate, *anglesite*, lead sulphate, and *celestine*, strontium sulphate are collectors' items and too soft for normal use. *Scheelite*, calcium tungstate, has been cut; two specimens are shown here, from Mexico and California, U.S.A. Synthetic scheelite has been used as a diamond simulant.

Turquoise (CASE 10A)

Hardness, 6; Specific gravity, 2.8–2.6.

The mineral consists of hydrous phosphate of aluminium coloured by copper which is present in varying quantities; small amounts of iron, also, are frequently revealed by analysis, and it has been suggested that the colouration is due to the complex ion formed by copper and ammonium. Turquoise is quite opaque and is valued for its colour alone, which, in the best and rarest specimens, is an intense sky-blue; greenish blue, apple-green, and greyish green material is commoner. It sometimes happens that a deeply coloured specimen tends to become much paler when exposed to sunlight, and stones that possessed a fine colour in the moist surroundings of the mine often become bleached and valueless when brought to the surface and dried. The original colour can be temporarily restored by placing such turquoise in damp earth, and this trick is sometimes resorted to in order to deceive intending purchasers. Immersion in a solution of ammonia will sometimes restore the blue colour to a stone which has become green, but, as in the former case, the improvement is not permanent. Pale turquoise is sometimes stained blue in the same way as agate (p. 63), but, if a drop of ammonia is placed on the back of such a stone, the spot becomes green or colourless, and the device easily detected.

Turquoise is never found in coarse crystals, but always in veins or infilling cavities in the country rock, which may be igneous or sedimentary. When thin sections are examined under the microscope, they are seen to consist of innumerable grains or fibres which are doubly refracting and consequently crystalline; like chalcedony, turquoise is micro- or crypto-crystalline. The hardness is low for a gemstone, but turquoise will always scratch glass, although it yields to a file.

Most of the specimens shown here are cut *en cabochon*, but flat stones engraved with gilt characters are exhibited, a method of treatment which is specially common in eastern countries where the turquoise is highly prized.

Most of the well-known localities for this mineral are illustrated here and a good series is exhibited from the Sinai Peninsula. The specimens came from the Wadi Meghara and were presented by Major C. K. Macdonald who rediscovered the mines at that place in 1845. These were worked in ancient Egyptian times but had been completely forgotten for many centuries. Here the turquoise occurs filling seams and cavities in a ferruginous sandstone.

Iran has long been renowned for its turquoise, the best known mines being situated near Nishapur, in the province of Khorassan. The village of Maaden is the centre of the mining, where the home of the turquoise is a porphyritic trachyte which pierces limestones, sandstones and slates. In places this trachyte forms a breccia cemented by limonite, with which the precious material is closely associated.

The detrital deposits from the weathering of the igneous rock are also exploited.

New Mexico has also produced good stones, and specimens are shown from Mount Chalchihuitl, Los Cerillos, Santa Fé Co., where the turquoise is found in porphyritic andesites which have been bleached and mineralised by the influence of volcanic vapours. Other places in this state have also yielded turquoise, particularly the Burro Mountains, in Grant Co., where it occurs in a decomposed granite, and also in Jarilla Mountains in Otero Co., where trachyte is the parent rock. Synthetic turquoise manufactured and presented by Pierre Gilson is also shown.

One or two stones are placed here which resemble turquoise in composition and are sometimes confused with it.

Variscite (hardness, $4\frac{1}{2}$–$5\frac{1}{2}$; specific gravity, 2.4–2.7) is a hydrated phosphate of aluminium having an apple-green or emerald-green colour. It has a vitreous lustre, takes on a good polish, and has sometimes been cut *en cabochon* for jewellery. It can be distinguished from turquoise by its lower hardness and specific gravity. The refractive index varies and is often difficult to determine. Specimens are shown from Utah, U.S.A., where the variscite occurs as nodules in a crystalline limestone.

Odontolite is simply fossil-bone stained blue or green by phosphate of iron. It can be distinguished from turquoise by the fact that it is heavier and shows traces of organic structure.

Howlite is a silico-borate of calcium which can be stained blue, and occurs in large quantities in the U.S.A.

Apatite (CASE 10A)

Hardness, 5; Specific gravity, 3.22–3.17; Doubly refracting; Refractive Index, 1.64; Birefringence, 0.003.

Owing to its soft nature, apatite is seldom used in jewellery. It consists of a complex fluophosphate of calcium and is commonly found in an impure form in rocks.

Pure apatite would be colourless, but gem quality material may be yellow, green, blue or violet. The crystals belong to the hexagonal class, and typically form hexagonal pyramids terminated by the basal plane. Several cut specimens are shown, including one from Portland, Quebec, Canada, presented by H.M. Queen Mary.

Brazilianite (CASE 10A)

Hardness, $5\frac{1}{2}$; Specific gravity, 2.99–2.98; Doubly refracting; Refractive Index, 1.62–1.60; Birefringence, 0.020.

Brazilianite was discovered in Minas Gerais, Brazil during 1944. It is a hydrous sodium aluminium phosphate so is related to turquoise and amblygonite; the colour is usually a curious greenish yellow. The monoclinic crystals are commonly prismatic.

Amblygonite (CASE 10A)

Hardness, 6; Specific gravity, 3.03–3.01; Doubly refracting; Refractive Index, 1.64–1.61; Birefringence, 0.026.

Amblygonite, usually yellow or colourless, is a fluophosphate of aluminium and lithium which crystallises in the triclinic system; the localities for it are Sao Paulo and Minas Gerais, Brazil. It has also been found in California and Maine in the U.S.A.

Beryllonite (CASE 10A)

Hardness, 6; Specific gravity, 2.84–2.80; Doubly refracting; Refractive Index, 1.56–1.55; Birefringence, 0.012.

This mineral, which is very rarely used as a gemstone, consists of a phosphate of sodium and beryllium, and crystallises in the orthorhombic system. Beryllonite occurs in colourless crystals, associated with phenakite in a granitic vein at Stoneham, Maine, U.S.A.

Phosphophyllite (CASE 10A)

Hardness, $3\frac{1}{2}$; Specific gravity, 3.1; Doubly refracting; Refractive Index, 1.62–1.60; Birefringence, 0.021.

This mineral, which is a zinc phosphate and crystallises in the monoclinic system, has an unusual bluish green colour and comes from Bolivia. It is too soft for normal use as a gemstone.

Lazulite (CASE 10A)

Hardness, $5\frac{1}{2}$; Specific gravity, 3.1; Doubly refracting; Refractive Index, 1.65–1.62; Birefringence, 0.036.

Lazulite, an iron magnesium aluminium phosphate (not to be confused with lazurite, which is a component of lapis lazuli), is of a blue colour but is rarely used for faceting or for ornamental work. Specimens shown here are from Brazil and Georgia, U.S.A.

Hambergite (CASE 10A)

Hardness, $7\frac{1}{2}$; Specific gravity, 2.4–2.35; Doubly refracting; Refractive Index, 1.63–1.55; Birefringence, 0.072.

The rare mineral hambergite is a hydroxy-borate of beryllium found only in southern Norway and Madagascar. It has a very large birefringence and a low specific gravity. The only value of the stone lies in its rarity, as otherwise it resembles quartz in appearance.

Amber (CASE 11A)

Unlike the other minerals described in this guide, this material is of organic origin.

Amber is the fossilised resin which came from coniferous trees growing in Lower Tertiary times. The small insects occasionally found embedded in it clearly prove its terrestrial origin.

Chemically, amber is composed of hydrocarbons, different varieties varying slightly in composition. The colour varies from yellow to brown: Baltic amber is commonly yellow, whilst Sicilian and Roumanian amber are usually of a darker shade. The hardness is from $2\frac{1}{2}$–3 and the specific gravity 1.05–1.1. Its property of becoming electrified when it is rubbed has been known since ancient times.

Various substitutes have been employed in place of amber, principally ambroid, kauri gum, and plastics.

Ambroid, or *pressed amber*, is made by heating small pieces of amber and pressing them together so that they coalesce. It may be distinguished from true amber by a 'flow' structure and by elongate bubbles. *Kauri gum* or *copal resin*, a recent resin from the Kauri-pine extensively found in New Zealand, is of similar specific gravity to amber, but may be distinguished by its easy fusibility. This may be tested by touching it with a hot needle, when it melts far more readily than amber. It is best to carry out a comparative test on real amber at the same time.

Most synthetic plastic imitations can be distinguished by their higher specific gravity, usually 1.25 or more. In a strong brine solution amber will float whereas these plastics will sink.

Amber should not be confused with the material *ambergris*, which is obtained from the intestine of the sperm whale for use in perfumes.

The main sources of amber are along the south-eastern coast of the Baltic Sea, and in Sicily, Roumania, Burma and Mexico. In the Baltic, which is by far the chief source, the principal locality is on the east side of the Gulf of Danzig, where the amber occurs in Oligocene beds. Occasionally amber has been washed up on the coast of East Anglia, probably from Lower Tertiary beds buried beneath the North Sea.

Jet (CASE 12A)

Also of organic origin, jet is a black variety of lignite or brown coal with a specific gravity of about 1.3, and a hardness of 3–4. It occurs in the Liassic shales of the Yorkshire coast near Whitby, and was worked for jewellery in the last century. Jet has also been imported from Spain and Turkey.

Ivory (CASE 12A)

Ivory is the name given to teeth or tusks of such mammals as elephant, mammoth, walrus, narwhal, hippopotamus, boar and cachalot whale which can be fashioned into ornaments. They are largely composed of dentine, chemically a calcium phosphate near hydroxyapatite in composition; the proportion of mineral to organic matter varies.

The specific gravity of elephant ivory lies between 1.90 and 1.70; the hardness ranges from $2\frac{3}{4}$ to $2\frac{1}{4}$. The intersecting lines 'lines of Retzius' in elephant ivory serve to distinguish it from bone and other types of ivory. Walrus ivory consists of two differing textures, well demonstrated by specimens in the case.

Bone can be identified by the fine tubes, Haversian canals, which may be seen.

Corozo nuts from the Ivory Palm and Doom Palm nuts are sometimes worked into vegetable 'ivory'.

Celluloid and plastic imitations have been widely manufactured.

Pearl (CASE 12A)

Pearls are nacreous concretions formed round an irritating nucleus in members of the Mollusca including oysters and mussels. The most important genus is Pinctada; freshwater pearls come from mussels such as Margaritifera; the giant conch (*Strombus gigas*) produces pink pearls without a pearly lustre.

Natural pearls are formed by the soft parts of the animal and are built up of layers of aragonite (calcium carbonate) and the organic substance conchiolin. The composition varies and with it the specific gravity which ranges from 2.78 to 2.60.

The iridescence ('orient') of the pearl is caused by the interference of light reflecting from the boundaries of translucent layers and also from the diffraction of light resulting from the closely packed ridges and grooves where the layers break surface.

The cultured pearl industry has been developed rapidly of recent years, mainly by the Japanese. As well as the method of placing a mother of pearl bead with a portion of the mantle of one animal into the shell of another they use a method whereby small portions of the mantle, carefully inserted, may produce a non-nucleated pearl; such are the Biwa pearls, from mussels farmed in the freshwater Lake Biwa in Japan. They take several years to grow to the requisite size.

Pearl fishing has been carried on from antiquity. Some areas, which are, or have been fished, are the Persian Gulf, the Red Sea, the Gulf of Manaar off Sri Lanka, around the shores of Burma, Malaysia, Borneo, Venezuela, Australia and Japan and other Pacific Islands.

APPENDIX

In order that the determination of the more important precious stones may be facilitated, a few tables have been inserted here. The stones have been classified according to colour and have then been arranged in order of specific gravity; other physical constants have been tabulated as it is necessary that some of these should be determined before a definite conclusion is arrived at as to the identity of a specimen. Only the transparent stones have been tabulated as it is with these that difficulty usually arises. The translucent and opaque stones, with one or two exceptions, can be readily determined, sometimes by mere inspection. Where there is a range of refractive indices this has been shown in the tables; the figures given do not, therefore, necessarily represent the maximum and minimum values for any particular stone.

Table 6 Colourless stones

Stone	Specific gravity	Hardness	Refraction	Refractive Indices
GGG	7.05	6	single	2.03
Scheelite	6.1–5.9	4½	double	1.94–1.92
Cubic zirconia	5.7	8½	single	2.18
Strontium titanate	5.13	6	single	2.41
Zircon	4.69	7½	double	1.99–1.92
Lithium niobate	4.64	6	double	2.30–2.21
YAG	4.57	8½	single	1.83
Synthetic rutile	4.25	6¼	double	2.90–2.62
Corundum	4.01–3.96	9	double	1.77–1.76
Synthetic spinel	3.63	8	single	1.73
Topaz	3.56	8	double	1.62–1.61
Diamond	3.52	10	single	2.42
Fluorspar	3.19–3.17	4	single	1.43
Euclase	3.10–3.05	7½	double	1.67–1.65
Tourmaline	3.04	7¼	double	1.64–1.62
Amblygonite	3.03–3.02	6	double	1.64–1.61
Danburite	3.00	7	double	1.64–1.63
Datolite	3.0–2.9	5	double	1.67–1.63
Phenakite	2.96	7¾	double	1.68–1.66
Pollucite	2.94–2.85	6½	double	1.53–1.51
Beryllonite	2.85–2.80	6	double	1.56–1.55
Calcite	2.71	3	double	1.65–1.49
Beryl	2.71–2.68	7¾	double	1.58–1.57
Rock crystal	2.65	7	double	1.55–1.54
Scapolite	2.63	6	double	1.55–1.54
Petalite	2.46–2.39	6	double	1.52–1.50
Hambergite	2.35	7½	double	1.63–1.55

Table 7   Red and pink stones

Stone	Specific gravity	Hardness	Refraction	Refractive Indices	Dichroism
Zircon	4.69	$7\frac{1}{2}$	double	1.97–1.92	not observable
Almandine	4.3–3.9	$7\frac{1}{4}$	single	1.81–1.75	absent
Spessartine	4.20–4.12	$7\frac{1}{4}$	single	1.80	absent
Ruby	4.0	9	double	1.77–1.76	distinct
Pyrope	3.8–3.7	$7\frac{1}{4}$	single	1.75–1.74	absent
Rhodochrosite	3.65–3.54	4	double	1.82–1.60	distinct
Spinel	3.65–3.58	8	single	1.72	absent
Topaz	3.53–3.50	8	double	1.64–1.63	distinct
Kunzite	3.18	$7–6\frac{1}{2}$	double	1.68–1.66	strong
Tourmaline	3.05	$7\frac{1}{4}$	double	1.64–1.62	strong
Morganite	2.90–2.70	$7\frac{3}{4}$	double	1.59–1.58	weak
Scapolite	2.67	6–5	double	1.57–1.55	distinct
Fire Opal	2.0	6	single	1.45	absent

Table 8   Yellow and brown stones

Stone	Specific gravity	Hardness	Refraction	Refractive Indices	Dichroism
Cassiterite	6.9	$6\frac{1}{2}$	double	2.09–1.99	distinct
Zircon	4.7–4.4	$7\frac{1}{2}$	double	1.97–1.92	not observable
Spessartine	4.20–4.12	$7\frac{1}{4}$	single	1.80	absent
Sphalerite	4.09	$4–3\frac{1}{2}$	single	2.37	absent
Corundum	4.0	9	double	1.77–1.76	weak
Chrysoberyl	3.74–3.64	$8\frac{1}{2}$	double	1.76–1.75	weak
Hessonite	3.65–3.63	7	single	1.74	absent
Topaz	3.54–3.50	8	double	1.64–1.63	distinct
Diamond	3.52	10	single	2.42	none
Sinhalite	3.52–3.46	$6\frac{1}{2}$	double	1.71–1.67	distinct
Epidote	3.5–3.35	$6\frac{1}{2}$	double	1.77–1.73	strong
Sphene	3.53–3.45	$5\frac{1}{2}$	double	2.06–1.91	distinct
Idocrase	3.4–3.3	$6\frac{1}{2}$	double	1.72	weak
Axinite	3.29–3.27	$7–6\frac{1}{2}$	double	1.69–1.68	strong
Apatite	3.22–3.17	5	double	1.64–1.63	weak
Spodumene	3.20–3.15	$7–6\frac{1}{2}$	double	1.68–1.66	weak
Andalusite	3.18–3.12	$7\frac{1}{2}$	double	1.64–1.63	strong
Fluorspar	3.18–3.02	4	single	1.43	absent
Tourmaline	3.11–3.05	$7\frac{1}{4}$	double	1.64–1.62	strong
Brazilianite	2.99–2.98	$5\frac{1}{2}$	double	1.62–1.60	weak
Beryl	2.71–2.68	$7\frac{3}{4}$	double	1.58–1.57	weak
Scapolite	2.70–2.68	6–5	double	1.57–1.55	weak
Quartz	2.65	7	double	1.55–1.54	distinct★
Orthoclase	2.56	6	double	1.53–1.52	absent

★ Only very weak dichroism in heat-treated stones.

Table 9 Green stones

Stone	Specific gravity	Hardness	Refraction	Refractive Indices	Dichroism
Zircon	4.69–3.94	7½–6	double	1.97–1.78	not observable
Corundum	4.0	9	double	1.77–1.76	distinct
Demantoid	3.86–3.81	6½	single	1.90	absent
Alexandrite	3.74–3.64	8½	double	1.76–1.75	strong
Epidote	3.50–3.35	6½	double	1.77–1.73	strong
Idocrase	3.4–3.3	6½	double	1.72–1.71	weak
Olivine	3.46–3.35	7–6½	double	1.69–1.65	weak
Kornerupine	3.35–3.28	6½	double	1.68–1.67	distinct
Diopside	3.31–3.27	6–5	double	1.70–1.67	very weak
Ekanite	3.28	6½–6	single	1.60	absent
Enstatite	3.27–3.1	5½	double	1.67–1.66	weak
Hiddenite	3.20–3.15	7–6½	double	1.68–1.66	distinct
Andalusite	3.18–3.12	7½	double	1.64–1.63	strong
Fluorspar	3.18–3.02	4	single	1.43	absent
Tourmaline	3.11–3.05	7½–7	double	1.64–1.62	strong
Euclase	3.10–3.05	7½	double	1.67–1.65	distinct
Phosphophyllite	3.1	3½	double	1.62–1.60	weak
Prehnite	2.94–2.88	6	double	1.64–1.61	very weak
Emerald	2.77–2.68	8–7½	double	1.58–1.57	distinct
Aquamarine	2.71–2.68	8–7½	double	1.58–1.57	distinct

Table 10 Blue stones

Stone	Specific gravity	Hardness	Refraction	Refractive Indices	Dichroism
Zircon	4.69	7½	double	1.97–1.92	strong
Sapphire	4.0	9	double	1.77–1.76	strong
Kyanite	3.68–3.60	7–5	double	1.73–1.72	distinct
Benitoite	3.68–3.64	6½	double	1.80–1.76	strong
Spinel★	3.65–3.58	8	single	1.72	absent
Topaz	3.57–3.56	8	double	1.63–1.62	weak
Zoisite	3.35	6½	double	1.70–1.69	strong
Fibrolite	3.25	7½	double	1.68–1.66	strong
Apatite	3.22–3.17	5	double	1.64–1.63	distinct
Tourmaline	3.11–3.05	7½–7	double	1.64–1.62	strong
Aquamarine	2.71–2.68	7¾	double	1.58–1.57	weak
Cordierite	2.65–2.58	7½–7	double	1.55–1.54	strong
Sodalite	2.28	6–5½	single	1.48	absent

★ Gahnospinel: Specific gravity 3.98, refractive index 1.747.

Table 11 Purple and violet stones

Stone	Specific gravity	Hardness	Refraction	Refractive Indices	Dichroism
Almandine	4.3–3.9	$7\frac{1}{4}$	single	1.81–1.75	absent
Corundum	4.0	9	double	1.77–1.76	distinct
Spinel	3.65–3.58	8	single	1.72	absent
Taaffeite	3.61–3.60	8	double	1.72–1.71	not observed
Kunzite	3.18	$7–6\frac{1}{2}$	double	1.68–1.66	strong
Fluorspar	3.18–3.02	4	single	1.43	absent
Scapolite	2.70–2.63	6–5	double	1.57–1.55	strong
Amethyst	2.65	7	double	1.55–1.54	distinct

INDEX

Absorption bands 15
Achroite 39
Actinolite 56
Adamantine lustre 8
Adularescence 16
Adularia 47, 59
Agate 65, 66
Alabaster 68
Albite 59
Alexandrite 41
Almandine 50
Amazonstone 59
Amber 71, 72
Ambergris 72
Amblygonite 71
Ambroid 72
Amethyst 63, 64
Andalusite 46, 47
ANDERSON, B. W. 40
Andradite 51
Anglesite 69
Anomalous double refraction 12
Anorthite 59
Apatite 70
Aquamarine 38
Aragonite 73
Artificial stones 26
Asterism 16
Australites 58
Aventurine feldspar 59, 60, 64
— glass 64
— quartz 64
Axinite 52

Barytes 69
Beilby layer 23
Benitoite 52
Beryl 37, 38
Beryllonite 71
Bezel facet 19
Biaxial minerals 12
Black opal 61
Blood-stone 65
Blue ground 34
'Blue John' 68
Bort 34

Boule 28
Bowenite 57
'Brazilian chrysolite' 39
'Brazilian emerald' 39
Brazilianite 70
Brilliant cut 19
Briolette cut 21
'Bristol diamonds' 63
Bromoform 6
Bronzite 54
Bruting 22
'Buxton diamonds' 63

Cabochon cut 22
Cairngorm 63
Calcite 63, 68
'Cape ruby' 49
Carat 2
Carbonado 33
Carborundum 22
Carbuncle 50
Carnelian 66
Carnelian-agate 65
Cascalho 33
Cassiterite 42
Cat's-eye 16
— chrysoberyl 41
— quartz 64
Celestine 69
Cerussite 68
'Ceylon' chrysolite 39
Ceylonite 40
Chalcedonic silica 65, 66
Chalcedony 65
Chalcedony-agate 65
Chatoyancy 16
'Chelsea' colour filter 15
Chemical properties 18
Chrysoberyl 41, 42
Chrysolite 44
Chrysoprase 65
Cinnamon-stone 50
Citrine 63
Cleavage 3
Clerici solution 6
Colour 14

Copal resin   72
Cordierite   51
'Cornish diamonds'   63
Corundum   35, 36
Critical angle   8
Crocidolite   64
Cross facets   19, 20
Crown of stone   19, 20
Crystalline form   3
Culasse of stone   19
Culet of stone   20
'Cullinan' diamond   35
Cutting gemstones   19
Cymophane   41, 64

Danburite   58
Datolite   58
De Beers Company   33
Delessite   65
Demantoid   51
Dentelle of stone   21
Diamond   31–35
Diamond simulants   30, 32
Dichroism   15
Dichroite   51
Dichroscope   15
Diopside   52, 53
Dispersion   10
Dolomite   68
Dop   22, 23
Double cabochon   22
— refraction   11
— rose   21
Doublets   25
Dry diggings   33
Dumortierite   58
Dunite   44

Ekanite   46
Electrical properties   17
Emerald   37
Emery   22, 35
Enstatite   54
Epidote   47
Essonite   50
Euclase   40

Facets   19
'False topaz'   63
Feldspar   59, 60
FEIL, C.   26
Fibrolite   47
'Fire'   11
Fire opal   62
Flash opal   61
Fluorspar   68

Fracture   5
FREMY, E.   26
FRIEDLANDER, I.   29
Fuchsite   57

Gahnospinel   40
Garnet   48, 49
GGG, Gadolinium gallium 'garnet'
   30, 32
GILSON, P.   30, 62
Girdle   19
Glass, natural   58, 59
Golconda Mines   33
Golden beryl   37
Green earth   65
Grossular   50
Gypsum   68, 69

Hambergite   71
HANNAY, J. B.   29
Hardness   3
Harlequin opal   61
Hauyne   67
Heliodor   38
Heliotrope   65, 66
Hessonite   49, 50
Hiddenite   53
'High' zircon   45
Hollowed cabochon   22
'Hope Blue' diamond   33
'Hope' sapphire   28
Howlite   70
Hyacinth   45
Hyalite   61
Hydrogrossular   50
Hypersthene   54

Iceland spar   12
Idocrase   46
Imitation of gemstones   24
Indicolite   39
Iolite   51
Ivory   72
— vegetable   72

Jacinth   45
Jadeite Jade   54, 55
Jagersfontein   33
Jargoon   45
Jasper   65
Jasper-agate   65
Jet   72

Kauri gum   72
Kimberley   33
'Koh-i-Noor' diamond   33

Kornerupine   47
Kunzite   52, 53, 54
Kyanite   46

Labradorite   60
Lapis-lazuli   66, 67
Lazulite   71
Lazurite   67
'Lithia emerald'   53
Lithium niobate   30
'Low' zircon   45
Lozenge   19
Lustre   7

Magnesite   68
Malachite   68
Marble   68
Marquise cut   21
Meerschaum   57
Melanite   51
Methylene iodide   6
Microcline   59
Milk opal   61
Mixed cut   21
Mohs' Scale   4
Mocha stone   66
MOISSAN, H.   29
Moldavite   58
Moonstone   59
Morganite   37
Morion   63
Moss agate   65, 66

Nephrite jade   55, 56
Nicol prisms   12
'Normal' zircon   45

Obsidian   58
Odontolite   70
Oligoclase   60
Olivine   44, 57
Onyx   66
Onyx-marble   68
Opal   60, 61, 62
Optical properties   7
Optic axes   12
'Oriental amethyst'   36
'— cat's-eye'   64
'— topaz'   36
Orthoclase   59

Paste   24
Pavilion facet   20
— of stone   19
PAYNE, C. J.   40
Pearl   73

Pendeloque cut   21
Peridot   42, 44
Petalite   58
Phenakite   41
Phosphophyllite   71
Plagioclase   59, 60
Plasma   65
Pleonaste   40
Polarisers   12
Polarity   38
'Polaroid'   12
Pollucite   58
Precious opal   61
Prehnite   52, 57
Premier Mine, Pretoria   33
Pressed amber   72
Putty powder   22
Pyro-electricity   18, 38
Pyrope   49
Pyroxene   52, 53

Quartz   62, 63, 64
Quoin facets   19, 20

Rarity of gemstones   1
Reconstructed stones   27
Reef   34
Refraction   8
Refractive index   10
Refractometer   13
Rhodochrosite   68
Rhodonite   54
River diggings   33
Rock crystal   62, 63
Rose cut   20
Rose quartz   64
Rouge   22
Rubellite   39
Rubicelle   39
Ruby   35, 36

Sapphire   35, 36
Sard   65
Saussurite   55
Scapolite   57, 58
Schorl   38
Scheelite   69, 74
Sepiolite   57
Serpentine   57
Silica   60, 65
Sillimanite   47
Single refraction   8
Sinhalite   44
Skew facet   19
Skill facets   20

Slocum stones   62
Smaragdite   54
Smithsonite   68
SMITHSON TENNANT   31
Smoky quartz   63
Soapstone   57
Sodalite   67
'Spanish topaz'   63
Specific gravity   5
Spectroscopic properties   14
Spessartine   50
Sphalerite   41
Sphene   48
Spinel   39, 40
Spodumene   42, 53
Star facet   19
— ruby   36
— sapphire   36
Steatite   57
Step cut   20
Strass   24
Strontium titanate   30
Sunstone   60, 64
Synthetic emerald   30, 37
—lapis lazuli   30, 67
—opal   30
—quartz   62
—ruby   27
—rutile   30
—sapphire   28
—scheelite   30, 69
—spinel   28, 40
—turquoise   30, 70

Taaffeite   40
Tables:
    Dichroic gemstones   17
    Hardness   4
    Refractive indices   14
    Specific gravities   6
Talc   57

'Tanzanite'   48
Tektites   58
Templet facet   19
Thermal properties   17
Thulite   48
Tiki   56
Tiger eye   64
Tinstone   42
Topaz   42, 43
Topazolite   51
Total internal reflection   9
Tourmaline   38, 39
Transparency   7
Trap cut   20
Tremolite   56
Triplet   25
Tripoli   22
Tugtupite   67
Turquoise   69, 70

Ultramarine   67
Uniaxial minerals   12
'Uralian emerald'   51
Uvarovite   51

Variscite   70
Verdite   57
VERNEUIL   26
Vesuvianite   46
Violane   53

Water-sapphire   51

X-rays   7

YAG, Yttrium aluminium
    'garnet'   30, 32
Yellow ground   33

Zircon   45, 46
Zirconia, cubic   30
Zoisite   48

Printed in the UK for HMSO   Dd. 736169 C75 3/83